THE POWER OF CHOICE

God's Word Speaks Concerning

Light and Darkness

Truth and Lies

Life and Death

By

Barbara A. Chimiak

The Power of Choice

Copyright © 2021 Barbara A. Chimiak

All rights reserved.

Deeper Life Press

Other versions used: New King James Version, Modern English Version,

The Supernatural Bible, New Living Translation, Amplified Bible-Classic Edition.

I call heaven and earth to witness against you today, that I have set before you life and death, the blessing and the curse. So choose life in order that you may live, you and your descendants, by loving the LORD your God, by obeying His voice, and by holding fast to Him; for this is your life and the length of your days, that you may live in the land which the LORD swore to your fathers, to Abraham, Isaac, and Jacob, to give them.

Moses
Deuteronomy 30:19–20

And if it seems evil to you to serve the Lord, choose for yourselves this day whom you will serve, whether the gods which your fathers served that were on the other side of the River, or the gods of the Amorites, in whose land you dwell. But as for me and my house, we will serve the Lord.

Joshua
Joshua 24:15 NKJV

There is a way which seems right to a man, but its end is the way of death.

Solomon
Proverbs 16:25

I am the light of the world. Whoever follows Me will never walk in darkness, but will have the light of life.

Jesus Christ
Gospel of John 8:12

DEDICATION

This work is dedicated to

Jesus Christ who introduced me to God our Father.

Holy Spirit who kept me focused on Christ.

My husband Walter—his loving flexibility released me in my pursuit of Christ.

All our children, that they may walk in Truth, bringing joy to the heart of Abba and making my heart glad.

Those who will receive Christ as Savior—welcome to the Family.

Those whose appetite for Truth will increase—God bless your hunger and make it multiply.

INTRODUCTION

Friday, September 11, 2009 began the first of seven nights when the Spirit of God woke me at midnight. His instruction was that I write what He released to me. What unfolded was a clear picture of the contrast between light and darkness, truth and lies and life and death and their consequences. These prophetic portions are printed in italics.

As Creator, God's design is for His purposes to be fulfilled on Earth. As the Father of Jesus Christ, His desire is for a companion for His Son, faithful and pure, as a bride prepared for her husband; a many-membered unified people who are loyal to Jesus as Messiah and Lord of all.

The children of God's household are to be a true reflection of His heart as they are transformed within by the Holy Spirit. God has revealed a way for us to walk in this life, and His way is perfect.

In times past, God would move through His servants the prophets revealing His thoughts so that people would be prepared for what would transpire. It remains the same today. This is a display of His sovereignty, mercy and love for mankind. It will serve you well to consider God's Word and to revere Him as the Creator and Sustainer of all that exists. I have included many scriptures that support each prophetic segment. No prophetic word is perfect, but it reveals God's thoughts and intentions.

Each person will stand before God one day. There will be an accounting of each individual's life. God has given liberally to all who have asked. The gift of your life surrendered to Him will bring glory to His name, joy to your heart and a fulfillment of the plans and purposes hidden before the foundations of the world.

God gave to us His only begotten Son, Jesus Christ, that we might know the true and living God. Jesus said, "If you have seen Me, you have seen the Father." Can others say that about you concerning Christ? For all who say that they know Him must also walk as He walked. Let us give Him our lives in abandoned devotion so that others may know Him too.

If God is on our side who can stand against us? His grace is sufficient for our every need; His life is abundant and we have not been left as orphans. He is a faithful Father and covenant-keeping God who has promised never to forsake us, and He is not a man that He would lie.

FROM THE AUTHOR:

This work comes out of a relationship that has developed over 48 years of being cared for by my Heavenly Father, the Faithful One who knew me before I was conceived in my mother's womb and had a purpose for me to fulfill. I am still on that life's journey.

To my Savior, Jesus Christ, the One who is love and fills me with wonder. Jesus is the one who made the supreme sacrifice that I might be reconciled to God and come to know truth; living increasingly free from the lie that would seek to rob my life and purpose. And to Holy Spirit, the precise teacher, who with such patience and gentleness comforts and encourages me, giving me faith and strength to believe in the things I cannot see yet anticipate with hope.

I am grateful for every joyous or difficult life circumstance that drove me further into God's heart for truth, understanding, and strength. I am thankful for each loved one or enemy that the Father allowed to touch my life at different seasons in order that I might see my lack and my need for more of His love.

For every book and article I have read, each prayer meeting, Bible study, conference and school I attended; each song, movie and testimony which added to the storehouse God is building in me, I am and will be forever grateful.

My desire is that you will come to a deeper understanding of God's ways and truth that He gives to govern life. In a culture that seeks to micromanage our waking moments we are free-thinking individuals whom God has given the RIGHT OF CHOICE.

May you meditate on what is written here and weigh the difference. See the contrast of light and darkness, truth and lies, life and death from God's perspective. Choose Christ and the life He offers and enjoy a vibrant relationship with the true and living God.

INDEX

SECTION I

1

THE LIGHT IN THE DARKNESS

Then Jesus again spoke to them saying,
I am the light of the world; he who follows Me will not
walk in the darkness, but will have the Light of life.

John 8:12

*The lights, the lights, the lights are increasing ... lights in the
darkness; lights that the darkness cannot overcome.*

*My hand is upon those who fear Me above all. They shall hear.
They shall see. They shall be My expression of life in a world of
brokenness and destruction. The light will overcome in times of
turmoil.*

*The light shall not flicker nor be extinguished. Lights seen as on a
hill on a plain; clear, visible lights, shining bright in a dark
place. I will bring forth My light and this light will be bright
within those who follow Me.*

*I will light the path of the just. It will lead those in darkness to
the place of life. Security is found in the light.*

The righteous shall shine like the dawn; as bright lights in a dark place. My Presence will be upon those who know My name and revere Me. I will not be mocked. The path of the just is like the dawn, getting brighter and brighter till the full day.

Before the living God enters into the human heart and mind, that person is filled with darkness. Darkness is the result of sin and the absence of light. Only when Christ, the light of the world, is invited within will there be true ability to see reality in the natural and spiritual worlds.

The Bible says that the entry of God's Word brings light. Abiding in God's Word daily will lead a person to activate their faith and trust in Him. In times of personal turmoil, confidence in God's promise that He will never abandon you gives stability. Fear can paralyze. God tells us not to be afraid. Courage, confidence and peace will become part of your character and obvious to those around you.

God's grace will enable you to grow in the knowledge of God and continue to make right choices because your desire is to honor Him. Holy love, which comes from our Father's covenant-commitment to us, will replace our fear with faith, and the light of Christ's life will shine brightly within.

Are you growing in the revelation of God as He shines the light of His life upon you?

In Him was Life, and the Life was the Light of men. And the Light shines on in the darkness, for the darkness

has never overpowered it (put it out or absorbed it or appropriated it, and is unreceptive to it).

John 1:4–5 AMP

My sheep hear My voice, and I know them, and they follow Me...

John 10:27

Your word is a lamp to my feet and a light for my path. The entrance of Your words gives light; It gives understanding to the simple.

Psalm 119:105, 130 NKJ

The path of the righteous is like the light of dawn,

That shines brighter and brighter until the full day.

Proverbs 4:18

The people who were sitting in darkness saw a great light, and those who were sitting in the land and shadow of death, upon them a light dawned.

Matthew 4:16

Then the righteous will shine like the sun in the kingdom of their Father. He who has ears, let him hear.

Matthew 13:43

2

THE RIGHTEOUSNESS OF CREATOR-GOD-HOLY AND SOVEREIGN

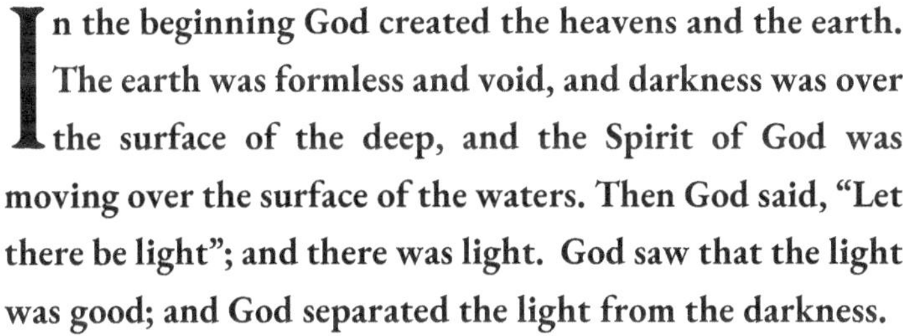

In the beginning God created the heavens and the earth. The earth was formless and void, and darkness was over the surface of the deep, and the Spirit of God was moving over the surface of the waters. Then God said, "Let there be light"; and there was light. God saw that the light was good; and God separated the light from the darkness.

Genesis 1:1–4

He put on righteousness like a breastplate, and a helmet of salvation on His head; and He put on the garments of vengeance for clothing and wrapped Himself with zeal as a mantle.

Isaiah 59:17

The righteous shall shine like the dawn; as bright lights in a dark place. My Presence will be upon those who know My name and revere Me. I will not be mocked.

Righteousness is like the dawn; it cannot be mistaken for darkness.

All lies will be exposed. Truth will prevail. Falsehood is like a sinking shard; it cannot keep itself afloat.

My Presence is like a thick curtain, weighty and all encompassing.

My senses will activate righteousness and justice in the earth. I will move. Who can stand against Me? I formed the sea. I created the light and the darkness.

I am above all. He who fears My name will walk on ground that is firm and unshakable. This person shall not be shaken, for I support all that concerns him. My Spirit shall not strive forever with the insolent.

Elohim, God our creator, gives us the gift of His righteousness so that we can choose to do what is right. Righteousness from God is not earned but imputed to the believer in Christ. Those who submit in humility to the Sovereign God, love His truth, and align with His character will be successful in all they do. The Holy Spirit teaches the follower to understand God's heart and reveals His ways.

Living and agreeing with biblical truth creates a distinction from those who live in agreement with worldly wisdom, deceitful scheming, selfishness, passing fads, traditions and lies. Our Father enables us to display His righteousness and strength in all circumstances. Walking in the fear of God will govern our actions and bring honor to Him.

Today, listen for God's words of righteousness and walk in the peace that comes from the solid foundation of the Scriptures.

For if by the one man's offense death reigned through the one, much more those who receive abundance of grace and of the gift of righteousness will reign in life through the One, Jesus Christ.

Romans 5:17 NKJV

Instead, we will speak the truth in love, growing in every way more and more like Christ, who is the head of his body, the church.

Ephesians 4:15 NLT

But He gives a greater grace. Therefore it says, God is opposed to the proud, but gives grace to the humble.

James 4:6

These six things the LORD hates, Yes, seven are an abomination to Him:

A proud look,

A lying tongue,

Hands that shed innocent blood,

A heart that devises wicked plans,

Feet that are swift in running to evil,

A false witness who speaks lies,

And one who sows discord among brethren.

Proverbs 6:16–19 NKJV

Those who have insight will shine brightly like the brightness of the expanse of heaven, and those who lead the many to righteousness, like the stars forever and ever.

Daniel 12:3

3

GOD OUR STRENGTH AND HELP

Who, then, is the man that fears the LORD?
He will instruct him in the way chosen for him.

Psalm 25:12

My forgiveness is readily available to the humble in heart. The proud remain in solitary, alone. Many are the trials of the righteous, but My faithfulness is their reward.

Those who cry over spilt milk will not see My glory; their eye is not on the prize.

Many, I say many are the sufferings of those who desire to know Me; but their portion shall not be taken away, nor shall it spoil in the time of adversity.

Many, I say many, are those who know My name and have not given themselves to falsehood.

You are not to fear.

I will part waters for you and you shall walk on dry land; I will see you through the dark times. My Presence will light your path. You will be a light in the darkness for those who will need to follow.

By faith we put our confidence in the unseen God. When we see His awesome work, we learn to reverently hold Him in the highest place of honor. God rewards our faith by giving us revelation of Himself, and we grow in the grace and the knowledge of the one true God, learning His ways as we experience His love for us.

This gives us an honest estimation of God and how He values each individual. We are called to love and treat others the same way that God has loved and treated us. We can easily get caught up in trivial things that take our focus off Christ. Maintaining relationship with Him must be our main goal. There are many good things we can enjoy, and I am thankful for each; yet there remains the need to prioritize our time, devotion, energy, and financial resources so that we keep the main thing, knowing God in Christ, our priority.

Others may not understand our faith; they may criticize our choices, and walk away. Loss is part of the journey. Our desire is to know God and grow in His likeness so that we honor Him and can be a genuine representation of His heart. This goal is each person's choice and privilege.

Fear of man can ensnare us. Fear of failure can hinder our on-going movement. Fear of the future can rob us of today's blessing. God is faithful to remind us of the eternal quest as we wholeheartedly humble ourselves and seek His way above every other way.

And the Spirit of the LORD will rest upon Him, the spirit of wisdom and understanding, the spirit of counsel and strength, the spirit of knowledge and the fear of the LORD. And He will delight in the fear of the LORD.

Isaiah 11:2–3a

For by grace you have been saved through faith; and that not of yourselves, it is the gift of God; not as a result of works, so that no one may boast.

Ephesians 2:8–9

You therefore, beloved, knowing this beforehand, be on your guard so that you are not carried away by the error of unprincipled men and fall from your own steadfastness, but grow in the grace and knowledge of our Lord and Savior Jesus Christ. To Him be the glory, both now and to the day of eternity. Amen.

2 Peter 3:17–18

Humble yourselves before the Lord, and he will lift you up.

James 4:10 NIV

Blessed is the man who perseveres under trial because, having stood the test, that person will receive the crown of life that the Lord has promised to those who love him.

James 1:12 NIV

I have set the LORD continually before me;

Because He is at my right hand, I will not be shaken.

Psalm 16:8

Peace I leave with you; My peace I give you; not as the world gives do I give to you. Do not let your heart be troubled, nor let it be fearful.

John 14:27

4

HOPE AND PEACE

❧

Return to the stronghold (of security and prosperity), you prisoners of hope; even today do I declare that I will restore double your former prosperity to you.

Zechariah 9:12 AMPC

Peace I leave with you, My peace I give to you; not as the world gives to you do I give to you. Let not your heart be troubled, neither let it be afraid.

John 14:27 NKJV

My people will be living containers of hope. In times of great desperation, hope will be alive and strong, an ever-living flame burning brightly within My people, My Beloved. You will know things others do not know. My people will be storage houses of information for life in the midst of turmoil.

My Peace is their stabilizer. Peace will cause them to stand, to walk, to persevere, to overcome, to triumph.

Higher I will take them above their enemies. They will ascend above the natural and know the way to go, what to do, why to turn this way and not that way. I will make the road safe where the enemy has set ambushes. My road markers will be clear and evident.

I will not fail those whose hope is in My unfailing love. My Word shall not return to Me void. I am not impotent.

The proud will receive the recompense of their doings; yet My mercy shall triumph over judgment. Be not deceived, I will not be mocked. Whatever one sows, that also will he reap. My Word is true. It is a lamp shining in a dark place.

Walking in humility is a virtue that can bring unexpected rewards. God promises to exalt those who have a humble attitude. Living daily in relationship with Him, we will walk in a fullness of life that others do not have. With Him we are aligned with Heaven, linked to the provision from above the natural. We may not have all that we desire because of our present circumstances, but if we have hope alive in our hearts, we will never be in despair.

Peace will enable us to persevere in trials and overcome the attacks of those who mock our faith. Each time we separate ourselves to be with God in His Word, He imparts holy substance. Peace can be tangible as we learn to trust His powerful indwelling life. This cannot be purchased from an online ministry or through fulfilling an obligation on special days of the year.

Time spent with the living God will always enrich our lives and prepare us to walk in His will; it's like making a withdrawal from God's heart and mind and depositing it into our being. Our minds will be changed and enlightened by the revelation and Presence of God's compassionate nearness.

The hope that God speaks about cannot disappoint us because it is the victorious Christ, living within, infusing His overcoming life through us to those around us.

Arise, shine; for your light has come, and the glory of the LORD has risen upon you.

Isaiah 60:1

Jesus answered them, 'To you it has been granted to know the mysteries of the kingdom of heaven, but to them it has not been granted.'

Matthew 13:11

Now may the God of hope fill you with all joy and peace in believing, so that you will abound in hope by the power of the Holy Spirit.

Romans 15:13

You are My friends if you do what I command you. No longer do I call you slaves, for the slave does not know what his master is doing; but I have called you friends, for all things that I have heard from My Father I have made known to you.

John 15:14–15

Do all things without complaining and disputing, that you may become blameless and harmless, children of God without fault in the midst of a crooked and perverse generation, among whom you shine as lights in the world, holding fast the word of life, so that I may rejoice in the day of Christ that I have not run in vain or labored in vain.

Philippians 2:15–16 NKJV

5

GOVERNMENT OF THE LIVING GOD

For a child will be born to us, a son will be given to us;
And the government will rest on His shoulders,

And His name will be called

Wonderful Counselor, Mighty God, Eternal Father, Prince of Peace.

Isaiah 9:6

All authority has been given to Me in heaven and on earth.

Matthew 28:18 NKJ

Pigs and dogs desire to devour. Call forth the shout of grace over My inheritance, My sons and daughters, and vanquish the darkness.

I will have My way in the earth.

My authority is given to those who overcome. My power will not be held back. The time is dawning for the day of reckoning.

My people will walk in the power purchased by My sacrificial blood.

I will strongly support all those who fear My name above all.

Man's frail attempts to usurp My place of authority will not purchase for them their spiritual inheritance. The work has already been completed. The purchase price paid. The document is sealed.

God's governing influence is enacted as the Holy Spirit prepares representatives, sons and daughters on Earth, and they are commissioned and sent. By God's grace choices are made to yield to Christ and live as He lived in God's truth so we may not be misled by error.

Christ was the first born of many who would follow in His footsteps. He walked among humanity declaring, "Repent, for the kingdom of heaven is at hand." God's authority is superior to human understanding; therefore, His kingdom will rule in the hearts and minds of those who respond to the Holy Spirit.

In scripture, pigs are unclean animals and dogs eat flesh, even dead flesh; they are scavengers. Dogs often referred to people who have dark intentions and plan to carry out evil, such as those who maliciously gossip to gain favor. God is holy and His people are commanded to be holy even as He is holy. The scriptures admonish us to be aware of the character of those we are in relationship with.

We are to understand that it is by God's grace we are able to see the darkness and choose to forsake its influence over us. By His grace (His ability in us) we gain by faith the enabling to overcome every sin, deception, and evil seduction, which are manifestations of darkness in the natural realm. United to Christ, we are called to walk above or overcome the natural, which is the higher standard of the Kingdom of God.

Fearing God above man and every worldly ploy opens the door of freedom to worship Him and to be confident of His ability in us without fear or shame. God honors those who put their life under His governing influence. Christ's blood has purchased us from the way of sin that leads to separation, captivity, and perdition. Our adoption as sons and daughters into God's family is complete. God sends those that He calls to be representatives of His kingdom; He gives angels assignments to keep them safe in all they do. It is a great privilege to bring His truth and Presence to those who are without hope, without God in this world.

Confidence is the earmark of those who are certain of God's covenant love; they will succeed in living under His government and releasing His authority in their sphere of influence.

For the eyes of the Lord move to and fro throughout the earth that He may strongly support those whose heart is completely His.

2 Chronicles 16:9a

Do not give what is holy to dogs, and do not throw your pearls before swine, or they will trample them under their feet, and turn and tear you to pieces.

Matthew 7:6

Now I say this, brethren, that flesh and blood cannot inherit the kingdom of God; nor does the perishable inherit the imperishable.

1 Corinthians 15:50

Be on your guard; stand firm in the faith; be courageous; be strong. Do everything in love.

1 Corinthians 16:13–14

Do not be overcome by evil, but overcome evil with good.

Romans 12:21

And I heard a loud voice in heaven, saying, 'Now the salvation, and the power, and the kingdom of our God and the authority of His Christ have come, for the accuser of our brethren has been thrown down, who accuses them before our God day and night. And they overcame him because of the blood of the Lamb and because of the word of their testimony, and they did not love their life even to death.'

Revelation 12:10–11

6

WHO IS LIKE OUR GOD?

**God is not a man, that He should lie, nor a son of man, that He should repent.
He has spoken, and will He not do it?**

Or has He spoken, and will He not make it good?

Numbers 23:19 MEV

I honor those who honor Me. I will not be mocked.

Many come in My name, but I have not sent them forth.

My brand, My mark is upon those who fear My name. My angels are given charge over them. Their watchmen never sleep. I am the Lord; I change not. You are the fragrance of life to those who are living and the fragrance of death to those who are perishing.

My Presence is as molten lava flowing.

The reality of the Creator-God has appeared and He makes Himself known through the life, death, resurrection and ascension of His Son, Christ Jesus. The powerful love of God was manifested through Jesus's sinless life; He honored, obeyed, and fulfilled His Father's will completely.

Those who walk in forgiveness and the love of truth will honor God. The life-flow of the resurrected Christ will manifest upon the earth through those who have yielded themselves to Him. When God's words pour from the mouth of those who are in covenant relationship with Christ, there is a life-flow of the glory of God that brings Heaven's realm and His Presence to Earth.

In the Old Testament, Moses obeyed and honored God before Pharaoh, the great king of Egypt, declaring God's will to release His people from Egyptian slavery. When Pharaoh sought to go after the people he had released, God performed a miracle by parting the Red Sea. All the people of God passed through to safety, but when Pharaoh's army pursued them, the sea closed over them and the entire army was drowned.

Be not deceived, God is not mocked. For whatever a man sows, that will he also reap.

Galatians 6:7 MEV

"If anyone serves Me, he must follow Me. Where I am, there will My servant be also. If anyone serves Me, the Father will honor him."

John 12:26 MEV

For I am the LORD, I do not change...

Malachi 3:6a MEV

Because you have made the LORD, who is my refuge, even the Most-High, your dwelling, there shall be no evil befall you, neither shall any plague come near your tent; for He shall give His angels charge over you to guard you in all your ways.

Psalm 91:9–11 MEV

To the one we are the fragrance of death, which brings death, and to the other the fragrance of life, which brings life. Who is sufficient for these things? For we are not as many are who peddle the word of God. Instead, being sent by God, we sincerely speak in Christ in the sight of God.

2 Corinthians 2:16–17 MEV

Section II

1
FAITH

Assuredly, I say to you, unless you are converted and become like children, you will by no means enter the kingdom of heaven.

Matthew 18:3

Childlike faith, innocent and expecting, is precious in My sight. So also are eyes that see beyond what is into what can be—creative, life-giving vision. Eyes that see beyond the immediate will bring forth My purpose.

Creativity will flow unhindered through union with the Creator. Each one born has a gift to employ. Fruitfulness is a mark of My Kingdom.

The waste places always have a purpose and the lush field is a delight to Me.

The rainbow has a remembrance, so also do the sunset and sunrise.

We are made in the image and after the likeness of the Creator-God. Everything He creates has a purpose even if it is just for His own pleasure. As we live in the flow of the Creator's life, His fingerprint will be seen through the various aspects of our daily living. By faith we have access to the heavenly realm and make it visible through our lives in a variety of ways.

Our lives are to be a reflection on Earth of the One we are connected with who is from above. We will be lovers of truth and hate lies. Integrity, honor, and respect will be given where they are due. Justice and compassion will be exercised upon all. Growth is an earmark of God's fruitfulness and purpose in and through those abandoned to Him by faith. Each season of life will help to develop God's intended goal in our new personality. He gives signs and lights in the skies to remind us of His power in the universe and written promises are found in the Scriptures.

Behold, I stand at the door and knock; if anyone hears My voice and opens the door, I will come in to him, and will dine with him, and he with Me.

Revelation 3:20

"Now faith is the substance of things hoped of, the evidence of things not seen."

Hebrews 11:1

My voice You shall hear in the morning, O LORD; in the morning I will direct it to You, and I will look up.

Psalm 5:3

I set My bow in the cloud, and it shall be for a sign of a covenant between Me and the earth.

Genesis 9:13

For by these He has granted to us His precious and magnificent promises, so that by them you may become partakers of the divine nature, having escaped the corruption that is in the world by lust.

2 Peter 1:4

2

PURPOSE

❧

But be self-controlled in all things, endure afflictions, do the work of an evangelist, and prove your ministry.

2 Timothy 4:5

There is a purpose to pursue and to fulfill. Life is meaningless apart from purpose.

My children shall lack nothing as they seek to fulfill their purpose. I am with you to enable you to excel in the earth for this next harvest season.

There is always a purpose; there is always a harvest. Multiplication is always a part of My economy. My purpose is full of life. Life, My life, is always multiplying and filling the earth with purpose.

Sons, born of love, strong and blessed with vision and purpose, shall never lack.

Purpose is like a choice field, purchased, plowed, prepared and tended; it will yield a bountiful harvest.

The river and the dry waste places need each other; both have a purpose. Ground that is parched needs preparation before it will receive its life; patience is a virtue, deep and strong in the parched places. He who walks in faith, united to the source of life, is all sufficient for every place.

Harvest is a joyous time; the labor is over and the purpose realized; this is the reward.

Marketplace evangelism brings much fruit. Bountiful is the harvest for the laboring harvesters, their reward is overflowing.

God's life is about productivity and abundance. United to God who is Love in the way He intends will bring forth His desires. The apostle Paul, formally known as Saul of Tarsus, knew that he had run the race of his faith and accomplished a bountiful harvest of souls for Christ. He fulfilled what God ordained for him to accomplish. When Jesus encountered Saul on the road to Damascus, Saul was on his way with an edict to capture more Christians, planning to imprison them. After he met the risen Messiah, Paul preached Christ, established churches, suffered untold agonies for his faith, and was inspired to write a large portion of the New Testament. He was a man who had experienced the resurrected Son of God. Paul's life was never the same. His name was changed, and he became one of

God's men in his day that would change history. The hardened heart was made new, filled with passion, and empowered to fulfill God's purpose in the earth.

We have the same opportunity to partner with our Father in His Kingdom and see the result of the Holy Spirit working through us to fulfill His good pleasure. However it is expressed, it will be a personal life-flow between you and God, affecting the world for good in your sphere of influence. There is a cost to fulfilling destiny, but the reward for the labor of faith brings joy that fuels our love for God and mankind.

I have fought the good fight, I have finished the race, I have kept the faith.

11 Timothy 4:7

And without faith it is impossible to please God, for he who comes to God must believe that He exists and that He is a rewarder of those who diligently seek Him.

Hebrews 11:6

He said to them, "The harvest truly is plentiful, but the laborers are few. Pray therefore the Lord of the harvest to send out laborers into His harvest."

Luke 10:2

We give no offense in anything, that our service may not be blamed. But in all things we commend ourselves as servants of God: in much patience, in afflictions, in

necessities, in distress, in stripes, in imprisonments, in tumults, in labors, in sleeplessness, and in hunger; by purity, by knowledge, by patience, by kindness, by the Holy Spirit, by genuine love, buy the word of truth, by the power of God, by the armor of righteousness on the right hand and on the left, by honor and dishonor, by evil report and good report, as deceivers, and yet true; as unknown, and yet well known; as dying, and look, we live; as punished but not killed; as sorrowful, yet always rejoicing; as poor, yet making many rich; and as having nothing, and yet possessing all things.

2 Corinthians 6:3–10

3

UNION

❧

I am the vine, you are the branches; he who abides in Me, and I in him, he bears much fruit; for apart from Me you can do nothing.

John 15:5

Union with Me brings union with each other, which brings forth My purpose in the Earth. One person is born with purpose to fulfill; each one needs another to succeed. Alone, *purpose is thwarted, even aborted.*

Union is key. Union brings forth life. Apart from Me you can do nothing; with Me the possibilities are endless. My purposes in the Earth shall be realized through those who have cultivated union.

My heart aches for intimate and honest relationship. I miss true fellowship with My children.

Cultivation of relationship will always produce a harvest. Love's roots go deep and spread wide, seeking the source of water to nourish. Always going deeper, wider, growing in the unseen place.

Relationship will not go unfulfilled. Union produces much. An earthly molecule is only one alone, but in union with the whole its purpose blooms with possibility. Pews are places where people sit. Without authentic union, a harvest is not possible.

My heart is satisfied through union.

Jesus said that He is the true vine and we are the branches. As we continue our relationship with Him in the Word, receiving from Him and enjoying fellowship with other believers and lovers of God, we will bring forth much fruit. What we do in life is not something apart from God's Spirit and the living provision of His servants in His body, the Church. We have been united to God through Christ and united to one another; together we will see God's purposes fulfilled.

Behold, how good and how pleasant it is for brothers to dwell together in unity! It is like precious oil upon the head, that runs down on the beard—even Aaron's beard—and going down to the collar of his garments; as the dew of Hermon, that descends upon the mountains of Zion, for there the LORD has commanded the blessing, even life forever.

Psalm 133:1–3 MEV

Your eyes have seen my unformed substance;
And in Your book were all written
The days that were ordained for me,
When as yet there was not one of them.

Psalm 139:16

Now faith is being sure of what we hope for and certain of what we do not see.

Hebrews 11:1

Believe me when I say that I am in the Father and the Father is in me; or at least believe on the evidence of the works themselves.

John 14:11

Just as a body, though one, has many parts, but all its many parts form one body, so it is with Christ. For we were all baptized by one Spirit so as to form one body, whether Jews or Gentiles, slave or free—and we were all given the one Spirit to drink. Even so the body is not made up of one part but of many.

1 Corinthians 12:12–14 NIV

Give thanks always for all things to God the Father in the name of our Lord Jesus Christ, being submissive to one another in the fear of God.

Ephesians 5:20–21 MEV

Be devoted to one another in brotherly love; give preference to one another in honor.

Romans 12:10

4

USURY

H e that by usury and unjust gain increases his substance, He shall gather it for him that will pity the poor.

Proverbs 28:8 KJV

Usury is an abomination in My sight. Unlawful gain will not go unpunished. I will not be mocked. I see every hidden thing; My heart abhors unjust gain. The oppressed shall not always go away empty; I will repay.

God's omniscience and omnipresent reality is in the Earth observing all the ways, thoughts, and motives of the heart of humanity. There are things He loves and things He hates. Strong words, yes; stronger yet is the reality of it. People may think that it doesn't matter what they think or do; they are ignorant of God's nearness. One day, they will be amazed by the One who has seen it all, every moment of every day of their life, and they will be abased before His holiness. Our prayer is that they would awaken to truth before it is too late.

You show love to thousands but bring the punishment for the parents' sins into the laps of their children after them. Great and mighty God, whose name is the LORD Almighty, great are your purposes and mighty are your deeds. Your eyes are open to the ways of all mankind; you reward each person according to their conduct and as their deeds deserve.

Jeremiah 32:18–19 NIV

5

CULTIVATION

~

Now it came to pass in those days that He went out to the mountain to pray, and continued all night in prayer to God.

Luke 6:12

There is much to be found in silence, in solitude. Relationship is cultivated in the unseen place, far from the crowd, gathering, searching, waiting, longing. This seeker's heart will not go unfilled. I will surely see and fill their treasuries.

The well, carefully dug, will bring forth much use. Water is necessary for life. A field without adequate water will never be much use in producing a crop. In My economy the well is never dry. I am the source of the water of life.

A field is useless without a well. Plan and dig wisely. Become a vessel.

My field is the world. My eye is upon the field. My desire will be realized in the field, for My purpose cannot be hindered.

My offspring are My economy in the world for the world. Prepared vessels accomplish much.

In order to hear a whisper silence is imperative. To develop any relationship, time spent together is needed; without quality time there can be no true heart connection. There is much activity in our daily existence. There are sounds that fill our mind, sounds that are different from many sources that are difficult to silence.

Christ set the example of making time to be alone with His Father. When we consider His ability to bring forth Kingdom power over the realm of darkness, how could we want anything less?

Behold, You desire truth in the inward parts,

And in the hidden part You make me to know wisdom.

Psalm 51:6 NKJV

Trust in the LORD, and do good; Dwell in the land and cultivate faithfulness. Delight yourself in the LORD; And He shall give you the desires of your heart.

Psalm 37:3–4 NKJV

And I will give you the treasures of darkness and hidden riches of secret places so that you may know that I, the LORD, who calls you by your name, am the God of Israel.

Isaiah 45:3 MEV

He said to me, "It is done. I am the Alpha and the Omega, the Beginning and the End. I will give of the spring of the water of life to him who thirsts."

Revelation 21:6 MEV

Therefore with joy you shall draw water out of the wells of salvation.

Isaiah 12:3 MEV

Jesus said to her, "Everyone who drinks of this water will thirst again, but whoever drinks of the water that I shall give him will never thirst. Indeed, the water that I shall give him will become in him a well of water springing up into eternal life."

John 4:13–14 MEV

SECTION III

1

THE NIGHT OF THE DEAD

J esus said to him,
**"I am the way and the truth and the life; no one comes
to the Father except through Me."**

John 14:6

*Life and death are in the power of the tongue. My life has
overcome the grave. Death could not overcome My life.
Resurrected life, My overcoming life is seen in the faith of those
who trust and believe.*

*Overcoming the grave brings forth the flow of life, which cannot
be quenched. Bursting forth out of death are all who put their
trust in the One who died and rose again, triumphing over death
and the grave.*

*My overcoming life is above the natural; it is supernatural. My
life operates by another life standard. Death reigns where sin*

thrives. Ever increasing and expanding is the life force of the power of sin and death.

Many say that they see, yet their sight is not true. Truth is seen in life. Death propagates the lie. The lie is rooted in sin, transgression and iniquity.

My life has overcome sin, death and the grave. The law of the spirit of My overcoming life is that which triumphs over sin. Sin breeds death. I am the Lord of life.

Jesus is the truth-teller. Only in Christ Jesus can the revelation of heavenly truth be realized. A person either is living under the power of sin and death, unable to understand biblical truth, or they have been quickened by the Holy Spirit and are living in the flow of divine life. By divine revelation, there is a dawning of truth that awakens the soul to the higher realm of life in the Spirit, which is superior to the natural life. The thirsting soul seeks to be satisfied, searching for that which is genuine. The awakening of truth must come from the One who is Truth.

As God draws people out of darkness, the light of truth shines on the path that leads to life. Victorious life has overcome the plan that leads to death--separation from God's life. The One who wears the Victor's Crown has triumphed over every lie that deceives, every power that enslaves, and the bondage that brings people into the captivity of darkness. The Holy Spirit has been given to us to enable us to become overcomers in Christ Jesus. When a choice is made to forsake old sinful thoughts and ways and begin to live united with the power of His indwelling life, our character is changed into Christlikeness—the ability to live as Christ did while on Earth.

When truth is spoken, the environment can change; situations can be seen from a different perspective, and light and life are realized.

The power of truth brings enlightenment. We no longer are slaves to sin. Romans chapter 8 gives clear directives. Freedom to forsake sinful thoughts and actions opens the door to freedom. Sin had no power over Jesus as He walked in obedience to God's Word. Free people are those who align with Heaven's truth. Can you see the way of escape from the power of sin and death by obeying the truth, honoring God, bringing joy to His heart and freedom to your soul?

Death and life are in the power of the tongue, and those who love it will eat its fruit.

Proverbs 18:21 MEV

In the beginning was the Word, and the Word was with God, and the Word was God. He was in the beginning with God. All things were created through Him, and without Him nothing was created that was created. In Him was life, and the life was the light of mankind. The light shines in darkness, but the darkness has not overcome it.

John 1:1–5 MEV

Jesus answered him, 'I assure you, most solemnly I tell you, that unless a person is born again (anew, from above), he cannot ever see (know, be acquainted with, and experience) the Kingdom of God.'

John 3:3 AMP

But when He, the Spirit of Truth (the Truth-giving Spirit) comes, He will guide you into all the Truth (the whole, full Truth). For He will not speak His own message, (on His own authority); but He will tell whatever He hears (from the Father; He will give the message that has been given to Him), and He will announce and declare to you the things that are to come (that will happen in the future).

John 16:13 AMP

Therefore there is now no condemnation for those who are in Christ Jesus. For the law of the Spirit of life in Christ Jesus has set you free from the law of sin and death.

Romans 8:1–2

Therefore if anyone is in Christ (that is, grafted in, joined to Him by faith in Him as Savior), he is a new creature (reborn and renewed by the Holy Spirit); the old things (previous moral and spiritual condition) have passed away. Behold, new things have come (because spiritual awakening brings a new life).

2 Corinthians 5:17 AMP

O death, where is your victory? O death, where is your sting? The sting of death is sin, and the power of sin is the law; but thanks be to God, who gives us the victory through our Lord Jesus Christ.

1 Corinthians 15:55–57

"For since by a man came death, by a man also came the resurrection of the dead. For as in Adam all die, so also in Christ all shall be made alive."

1 Corinthians 15:21–22

This is the message we have heard from Him and announce to you, that God is light, and in Him there is no darkness at all.

1 John 1:5

2

THE OVERCOMER

In Him was life, and the life was the light of mankind. The light shines in darkness, but the darkness has not overcome it.

John 1:4–5 MEV

My life, My overcoming life has conquered death and the grave. Life in and from My life. Light is found in the darkness where I am. My life has overcome darkness. The flow of resurrection life cannot be thwarted. I act. Who can reverse it?

Man's pride refuses the light. It opposes truth and life. Where sin reigns lies are lord. My heart is the life source of the universe. I spoke and the worlds were formed. All life comes from Me. My life is more powerful than death. There is life in My life. Apart from Me there is no life; all is futility.

Men see, yet they are blind. Men speak, yet their words fail; they fall to the ground, failing to produce life. Oh pride, where is your ability to produce life? You reign in death. The flow of life begins in the Rock of Ages. Out of the rock water flowed; who could imagine such a thing?

In the waste places I watch, I wait to see a movement of faith. Life triumphs over death. Faith prevails over darkness. Above the storm is life. The root of life is faith.

Like molten lava is My life; moving, flowing, overcoming all. Nothing can stop My life flow. I have already overcome death. In Me is life; there is no darkness at all; death cannot reign where life has already taken root.

My life has overcome sin, death, and the grave. I act. Who can reverse it? Life comes forth as light from the tongue of the wise. The just speak life out of the treasure of faith.

When faith connects to heavenly realms and is united to the resurrected LORD, life's journey is more than mere existence. Life takes on meaning and purpose. Jesus has come, come to us to make us alive with Him. Jesus is our living hope. Eternity begins now. Many have yet to respond and begin to live in the overcoming life flow that the Messiah offers to those who believe in Him. Before Christ, I lived in the realm of darkness, sin, and death, which led to a vicious cycle of pain and disappointment. God came and enlightened my darkness revealing the option to choose light and life. Why would anyone want to live a day without Him? This is why Jesus is the Savior of all who believe in Him.

Indeed before the day was, I am He; And there is no one who can deliver out of My hand; I work, and who will reverse it?

Isaiah 43:13 NKJV

This is the verdict, that light has come into the world, and men loved darkness rather than light, because their deeds were evil. For everyone who does evil hates the light and does not come to the light, lest his deeds should be exposed. But he who does the truth comes to the light, that it may be revealed that his deeds have been done in God.

John 3:19–21 MEV

The LORD lives! Blessed by my Rock! Let God be exalted, The Rock of my salvation!

2 Samuel 22:47 NKJV

If I say, "Surely the darkness shall cover me, and the light shall be as night about me," even the darkness is not dark to You, but the night shines as the day, for the darkness is like light to You.

Psalm 139:11–12 MEV

Pride goes before destruction, and a haughty spirit before a fall.

Proverbs 16:18 NIV

Simon Peter answered Him, "Lord, to whom shall we go? You have the words of eternal life."

John 6:68 MEV

The thief comes only to steal and kill and destroy; I have come that they may have life, and have it to the full.

John 10:10

For the eyes of the LORD move to and fro throughout the earth that He may strongly support those whose heart is completely His. You have acted foolishly in this. Indeed, from now on you will surely have wars.

2 Chronicles 16:9

There is one who speaks rashly like the thrusts of a sword, but the tongue of the wise brings healing.

Proverbs 12:18

Jesus said to her, "I am the resurrection and the life; he who believes in Me will live even if he dies, and everyone who lives and believes in Me will never die. Do you believe this?"

John 11:25

For You light my lamp; The LORD my God illumines my darkness.

Psalm 18:28

But if the Spirit of Him who raised Jesus from the dead lives in you, He who raised Christ from the dead will also give life to your mortal bodies through His Spirit who dwells in you.

Romans 8:11 MEV

Behold, I will stand before you there on the rock in Horeb; and you shall strike the rock, and water will come out of it that the people may drink.

Exodus 17:6

3

LIES AND PRIDE

There is a way which seems right to a man, but its end is the way of death.

Proverbs 14:12

Oh tongue, where is your justification, your vindication? When you speak and exercise lies, death reigns. When others agree, you are strengthened. I watch and I weep. Oh, how vast is the grave of death; its roots go very deep. In darkness it breeds more lies; it grows, strengthened by agreement.

Break covenant with death, Oh peoples of the earth. Be not overcome by the sewer of lies. Even My own people have been swayed by lies. Many have bartered in the flow of death. Power-hungry pride exercises death over life. Truth is exchanged for the lie. For a season this seems good, yet the night of death awaits those who exchange truth for the lie. There is no life there. Only darkness flourishes in the light of lies.

And the LORD God planted a garden toward the east, in Eden, and there He placed the man whom He had formed. And out of the ground the LORD God caused to grow every tree that is pleasing to the sight and good for food, the tree of life also in the midst of the garden, and the tree of the knowledge of good and evil.

Genesis 2:8–9

Then the LORD God took the man and put him into the Garden of Eden to cultivate it and keep it. And the LORD God commanded the man, saying, 'From any tree of the garden you may eat freely; but from the tree of the knowledge of good and evil you shall not eat, for in the day that you eat from it you shall surely die.'

Gen. 2:15–17

He created them male and female, and He blessed them and named them Man in the day when they were created.

Gen. 5:2

God created the earth and everything that has life within itself—plant, animal and human. Various and unique in its creation with the ability to multiply after its own kind, each form is an expression of God's creativity; only mankind was made after the likeness of his Creator. Then God took the man, Adam, whom He had created, and placed him in a Garden where the man would begin to function in his purpose. He then gave Adam a command, exercising His right as the Sovereign. As

Creator, God has the foreknowledge to enable man to live and function to his highest potential as he receives instruction. It is the man's responsibility to conduct himself within the parameters of God's commands. Adam partnered with God's work in Eden. It is clear that God had given man the ability to choose as He permitted Adam to assign a name to each animal God had created.

During one of their daily encounters, God gave Adam the command that, if obeyed, had power to keep him in a place of security. At this point in Adam's life, he walked in peaceful fellowship with God; but this was about to change. God created Adam and Eve with the ability to willingly obey Him. There is always a consequence in disobeying a command of God, yet God's mercy is even greater than our disobedience.

One day, the serpent approached Eve and initiated conversation concerning The Tree of the Knowledge of Good and Evil of which God had said they were not to eat. He appealed to her reason and she gave in to cunning seduction. Satan countered God's commanded truth stating,

"You surely shall not die! For God knows that in the day you eat from it your eyes will be opened and you will be like God, knowing good from evil."

Genesis 3:4–5

Eve looked at the fruit and gave attention to the words of the arch enemy of all goodness, truth and life. She allowed her reasoning to be preeminent over God's Word and chose to embrace the word of the thief. Adam also agreed, partnering in the rebellion. At this moment in time, it seemed right for them to accept the serpent's statement. In the moment Adam and Eve received the lie as truth, the beautiful life that was a gift from Creator-God would be assaulted, and their sight was no longer pure. A door in man's soul had closed and another door had opened. A shift occurred that would affect every human being thereafter. Now, the result of words that rolled off the tongue of the Father of Lies would set in motion the law of the power of sin and death within every person born. Only divine wisdom and intervention could turn things around. Adam and Eve had forfeited their dominion to the devil, and they were in need of being saved and reconciled to God. The enemy of man's soul had gained victory over them, but God's ultimate plan would not be thwarted forever. He would bring a man who would not question His supreme authority and would not yield to the temptation of satanic influence. The Son of Man, Christ Jesus, would become the reconciling agent and the home of refuge and truth for all who believe.

May the LORD cut off all flattering lips, the tongue that speaks great things; who have said, 'With our tongue we will prevail; our lips are our own; who is lord over us?'

Psalm 12:3–4

The sorrows of those who have bartered for another god will be multiplied....

Psalm 16:4a

Therefore hear the word of the LORD, you scornful men, who rule this people who are in Jerusalem, because you have said,

"We have made a covenant with death, and with Sheol we are in agreement, When the overflowing scourge passes through, it will not come to us, for we have made lies our refuge, and under falsehood we have hidden ourselves."

Isaiah 28:14–15 NKJV

But if your eye is bad (spiritually blind), your whole body will be full of darkness (devoid of God's precepts). So If the (very) light inside you (your inner self, your heart, your conscience) is darkness, how great and terrible is that darkness!

Matthew 6:23 AMP

Do not be deceived, God is not mocked, for whatever a man sows, this he will also reap. For the one who sows to his own flesh will from the flesh reap corruption, but the one who sows to the Spirit will from the Spirit reap eternal life.

Galatians 6:7–8

Dear children, do not let anyone lead you astray. The one who does what is right is righteous, just as he is righteous. The one who does what is sinful is of the devil, because the devil has been sinning from the beginning. The reason the Son of God appeared was to destroy the devil's work.

1 John 3:7–8 NIV

Jesus said to him, I am the way, and the truth, and the life; no one comes to the Father but through Me.

John 14:6

4

THE SUPERIOR LAW

For the law of the Spirit of life in Christ Jesus has set you free from the law of sin and death.

Romans 8:2

Light is sown in the lives of those who love truth. Death has no dominion over them. They have ascended above death. They live out of My life. Union with Me brings forth life, transcending death's structure and death's alluring influence. The ascended life overcomes the law of sin and death. It is an ever-increasing life; its very source is rooted in God.

In Me is life and My life is the light of the world. I act. Who can reverse it?

A child is born. Life begins. The child grows and has potential. Who will control this new life? Will it be fed truth or lies? Life will multiply. Will truth or lies grow? Life issues forth and grows from the root. Whatever is planted will grow; its roots reaching deeper into the soil of its life.   The fruit of the tree will ultimately issue forth from the root system.

The law of sin and death was set in motion when Adam and Eve chose to forsake God's Word and accept the word of the serpent, which was a lie. God had commanded Adam not to eat from the Tree of the Knowledge of Good and Evil, telling him that if he did, he would die. Satan in the form of the serpent told Eve that she surely would not die.

God's Word is true; and if His Word is believed and followed, the result will always be life and peace. On this side of Heaven it is beneficial for us to know God's Word and to obey it.

Spiritual death was the consequence of disobedience. Accepting God's sacrifice for sin is the pathway of reconciliation with God, which issues from the law of the Spirit of life in Christ. Jesus told Nicodemus, who was a ruler of the Jewish people, that it would be necessary for him to be born again to see and experience the Kingdom of God. We then live our lives forsaking lies and embracing truth so that we may enjoy supernatural life.

Jesus answered, Truly, truly, I say to you, unless one is born of water and the Spirit, he cannot enter into the kingdom of God. That which is born of flesh is flesh, and that which is born of the Spirit is spirit. Do not marvel that I said to you, 'You must be born again.'

John 3:5–7

I am the way, the truth and the life. No one comes to the Father except through Me.

John 14:6 MEV

Abide in Me, and I in you. As the branch cannot bear fruit of itself unless it abides in the vine, so neither can you unless you abide in Me.

John 15:4

Sanctify them in the truth; Your word is truth.

John 17:17

If then you have been raised up with Christ, keep seeking the things above, where Christ is seated at the right hand of God. Set your mind on the things above not on the things that are on earth. For you have died and your life is hidden with Christ in God.

Colossians 3:1–3

Therefore consider the members of your earthly body as dead to immorality, impurity, passion, evil desire, and greed, which amounts to idolatry. For it is on account of these things that the wrath of God will come, and in them you also once walked, when you were living in them. But now you also, put them all aside: anger, wrath, malice, slander, and abusive speech from your mouth. Do not lie to one another, since you laid aside the old self with its evil practices, and have put on the new self who is being renewed to a true knowledge according to the image of the One who created him—a renewal in which there is no distinction between Greek and Jew, circumcised and uncircumcised, barbarian, Scythian, slave and freeman, but Christ is all, and in all.

Colossians 3:5–11

And we know that the Son of God has come, and has given us understanding so that we may know Him who is true; and we are in Him who is true, in His Son Jesus Christ. This is the true God and eternal life.

1 John 5:20

And out of the ground the LORD God caused to grow every tree that is pleasing to the sight and good for food; the tree of life also in the midst of the garden, and the tree of the knowledge of good and evil.

Genesis 2:9

For further reading: Genesis 2:15–17; 3:1–19

5

CHOICES

~

This is the verdict, that light has come into the world and men loved darkness rather than light, because their deeds were evil.

For everyone who does evil hates the light and does not come to the light, lest his deeds should be exposed.

John 3:19–20 MEV

The reign of death is coming to the time of fullness. The root of death has multiplied and spread across the Earth. Men have desired darkness instead of light.

Yet My day of triumph for those who have chosen and embraced life will burst forth upon the Earth bringing the reign of overcoming life and its consequences.

There is a consequence to every choice. Life and death is in the power of the tongue. Choose life and live. Truth will prevail; it cannot fail. Truth has overcome the lie. Death has been overcome by My life. Oh Death, where is thy victory; oh Death, where is thy sting? The power of death is the law. I have overcome with My life.

In the fullness of time, there will be a day when the power of sin and death will overcome many upon the earth. Individuals will make a choice concerning who they live to serve, self or God. By grace through faith, those who have chosen God will live in the victory of truth and life. Those who have chosen to reject Him will live for themselves and align with darkness and under the power of sin and death. Jesus has said that He is the way and the truth and the life. Each choice will carry the weight of its consequence.

Truly, truly I say to you, he who believes in Me will do the works that I do also. And he will do greater works than these, because I go to My Father.

John 14:12

Death and life are in the power of the tongue, and those who love it will eat its fruit.

Proverbs 18:21

For by your words you will be justified, and by your words you will be condemned.

Matthew 12:37 MEV

For from within, out of the heart of men, proceed the evil thoughts, fornications, thefts, murders, adulteries, deeds of coveting and wickedness, as well as deceit, sensuality, envy, slander, pride and foolishness. All these evil things proceed from within and defile the man.

Mark 7:21–23

I call heaven and earth to witness against you today, that I have set before you life and death, the blessing and the curse. So choose life in order that you may live, you and your descendants.

Deuteronomy 30:19 MEV

O death, where is your sting? O grave, where is your victory? The sting of death is sin, and the strength of sin is the law. But thanks be to God, who gives us the victory through our Lord Jesus Christ.

1 Corinthians 15:55–56 MEV

For by grace you have been saved through faith, and that not of yourselves, it is the gift of God, not of works, lest anyone should boast.

Ephesians 2:8–9 NKJV

For all that is in the world, the lust of the flesh and the lust of the eyes and the boastful pride of life, is not of the Father, but is from the world.

1 John 2:16

Whoever is wise, let him understand these things; whoever is prudent, let him know them. For the ways of the LORD are right, and the just will walk in them; but the transgressors stumble in them.

Hosea 14:9

SECTION IV

This Is Your God

1. The Fountain of Living Water
2. The One Who Calls
3. The One Who Saves
4. He Who Knows All and Loves Perfectly
5. Faithful God and Father, Lord and Lover of Mankind
6. The One Who Heals and Delivers, Moving in Wisdom and Insight, Mercy and Tenderness
7. The One Who Sees and Understands, Forgives and Restores
8. He Who Reconciles Sleeps Not
9. The One Who Knows the End from the Beginning
10. He Who Opens and No One Can Shut
11. He Who Inspires and Creates, Moves & Waits—Never Tires
12. Father, Mother, Brother, Friend, Savior, Spouse, Beloved, Desire of the Nations
13. Name above All Names, the High and Holy Majestic One, Ever-Present, All-Knowing, All-Powerful God
14. The Perfect One, Lacking Nothing, Possessor and Sustainer of All Things
15. The Fruitful One, the Vine
16. The Water of Life, He Who Cleanses

17. The Bread of Life, He Who Satisfies

18. The Light of the World, Our Teacher

19. The Unseen, Ever-Present One Who Fills the Earth with Goodness

20. The Gentle One Moving in Compassion

21. The Jealous Lover, Passionate and Protective

22. The Holy One Filled with All Knowledge

23. The Day-Star Who goes before His People Making the Crooked Straight and Leveling Every Exalted Place

24. He Who Sees Judges Not and Yet His judgment Is in the Earth

25. The Ever-flowing Stream Filled with Life, Nourishing the Earth

26. The One Who Shepherds, Guides and Corrects

27. The Beautiful Radiant One Who Fills the Earth with Song, Color and Beauty

28. The Relentless Lover Who Pursues and Overcomes

29. He Who Fills My Mouth with Good Things and Whose Strength Never Fails

30. The Light in the Darkness, the Flame that Cannot Be Extinguished

31. The Father of the Prodigal; the Lover of the Harlot; the Husband to the Widow and Father of the Orphan

32. The Head of the Body, the Pillar of Strength; Our Refuge and Strong Tower

33. The Defense against Our Enemies, Our Advocate

34. He Who Justifies

35. He Who Glorifies and Crowns His People with Loving Kindness and Mercy

36. He Who Empties and He Who Fills, the Eternal One
37. He Who Knows Every Hair on Our Head and Names Each Star
38. The Tender, Patient, All-Encompassing One, Upholding All Things with His Right Hand
39. The Captain of the Heavenly Host, the Mighty Warrior
40. Our Passover Lamb, Substitute and Victorious Triumphant One
41. Our Joyous Overcoming King and Prince of Peace
42. Hope of the Nations; King Above All Kings, Lord Above All Lords, The Exalted One
43. The One Who Gathers and He Who Scatters Is the Same
44. He Who Raises the Dead and Quickens the Fainting One, Opens Blind Eyes, Unplugs Deaf Ears , and Makes a Heart of Stone a Heart of Flesh—He Never Tires of Doing Good
45. He Will Not Be Mocked
46. He Is the Truth
47. He Never Fails, He's Already Overcome
48. He is the Alpha and the Omega, Giving Rest to the Weary, the Hope
49. He Grieves, He Weeps, He Gets Angry, He Rejoices and Laughs at His Enemies
50. The Sun of Righteousness, the Morning Star
51. The Son of God, His Name Is Jesus the Christ, God's Messiah, the Sent One, the Prophet
52. Who Restores the Soul, Our High Priest, the Priest of the Most-High God, Our Redeemer
53. Way, the Truth, the Life

1

THE FOUNTAIN OF LIVING WATER

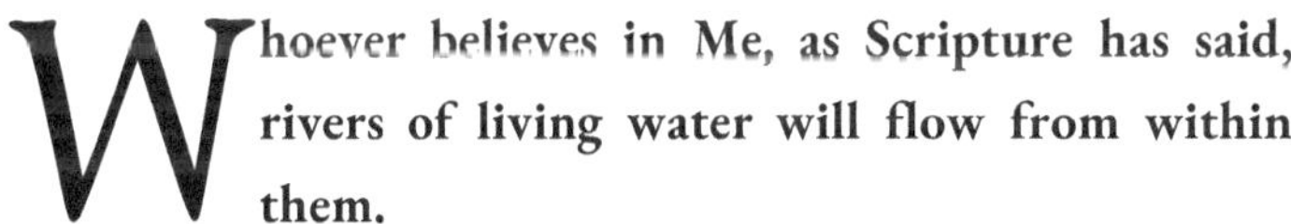

Whoever believes in Me, as Scripture has said, rivers of living water will flow from within them.

John 7:38 NIV

When we receive Christ as Lord, and His Spirit enters our spirit, we are making a place where He can be worshipped and known. In a sense we are building a throne for God to occupy. The Holy Spirit is to us the fullness of the Godhead. As He is working within us, He is changing us and establishing the character of God to bring forth our born-again personality. When we speak, we have the opportunity to allow our words to bring truth, refreshing and life. Clear, clean water brings cleansing and nourishment. As our life becomes an act of on-going worship, the water of spirit and life will flow from us to those who need to experience God.

Husbands, love your wives, just as Christ also loved the church and gave Himself up for her, so that He might sanctify her, having cleansed her by the washing of water with the word, that He might present to Himself the church in all her glory, having no spot or wrinkle or any such thing; but that she would be holy and blameless.

Ephesians 5:25–27

And he showed me a river of the water of life, clear as crystal, coming from the throne of God and of the Lamb, in the middle of its street. On either side of the river was the tree of life, bearing twelve kinds of fruit, yielding its fruit every month; and the leaves of the tree were for the healing of the nations.

Revelation 22:1-2

My people have committed two sins: They have forsaken me, the spring of living water, and have dug their own cisterns, broken cisterns that cannot hold water.

Jeremiah 2:13

2

THE ONE WHO CALLS

ut now, thus says the LORD, your Creator, O Jacob, And He who formed you, O Israel, 'Do not fear, for I have redeemed you;

I Have called you by name, you are Mine!'

Isaiah 43:1

The Creator of the world is the One in whose image we are created. He calls us to Himself to develop relationship. He reveals to us that we are not to be afraid because His love for us is perfect. Christ has reconciled us to God by His work on Calvary. God has already made a decision that He wants to be in relationship with us. This requires a decision from our heart to turn toward Him and not away from Him. When God calls our name, we have an opportunity to respond to His voice. He tells us that we are His and we belong to Him. No one can use reputation to get close to God. No one can pay a price to belong to God. The Creator-God is the one who paid the price to redeem us from the nature of sin through the death of His Son, that we may know Him, love Him, and enjoy Him.

Grace and peace be multiplied to you in the knowledge of God and of Jesus our Lord; seeing that His divine power has granted to us everything pertaining to life and godliness, through the true knowledge of Him who called us by His own glory and excellence.

2 Peter 1:2–3

And we have come to know and have believed the love which God has for us. God is love, and the one who abides in love abides in God, and God abides in us.

1 John 4:16

For those whom He foreknew, He also predestined to become conformed to the image of His Son, so that He would be the first born among many brethren; and these whom He predestined, He also called; and these whom He called, He also justified; and these whom He justified, He also glorified.

Romans 8:29-30

3

THE ONE WHO SAVES

I, even I, am the LORD; And there is no savior besides Me.

Isaiah 43:11

Before the Holy Spirit of God began to draw us to Himself, we were living in darkness, separated from the life of God, under the dominion of the power of sin and death. By grace the Gospel reveals Christ to be the only way of salvation; the only mediator between God and mankind. By faith we respond and receive new life in Christ Jesus. We have passed from death to life; the life God had intended for us before sin entered into humanity. God desires that none should live separated from Him but that all would come to the knowledge of the truth as the Scripture reveals concerning reconciliation.

For God so loved the world, that He gave His only begotten Son, that whoever believes in Him, should not perish, but have eternal life. For God did not send the Son into the world to judge the world, but that the world should be saved through Him.

John 3:16–17

4

HE WHO KNOWS ALL
AND LOVES PERFECTLY

For I know the plans that I have for you, declares the Lord, plans for welfare and not for calamity to give you a future and a hope.

Jeremiah 29:11

God's plans unfold when He is ready to do something new. Christ made His appearance upon the earth at the appointed time in history; so also, God has a time for us to come to know who He is. God's providence has made provision for every life, and His plan unfolds for us to recognize. Grace begins to operate in our mind and heart, stirring a desire that is yet to be fulfilled.

Declaring the end from the beginning, and from ancient times things which have not been done, saying, 'My purpose will be established, and I will accomplish all My good pleasure.'

Isaiah 46:10

For He Himself knows our frame; He is mindful that we are but dust.

Psalm 103:14

In that day you will ask in My name, and I do not say to you that I will request of the Father on your behalf; for the Father Himself loves you, because you have loved Me and have believed that I came forth from the Father.

John 16:26–27

5

FAITHFUL GOD AND FATHER, LORD AND LOVER OF MANKIND

God is faithful, who has called you into fellowship with His Son, Jesus Christ our Lord.

1 Corinthians 1:9

Because of the Lord's unconditional love for mankind, He didn't forsake His creation when they failed to obey Him. In His faithful love, He shed the blood of an innocent animal and made a covering for Adam and Eve's nakedness. A better and more perfect sacrifice would appear in the future that would seal man's protection against the penalty of sin forever. Like the blood of the Passover lamb, which was applied to the outside of the entryway of the houses of the Jewish people in Egypt that kept the death angel away, the blood that Christ shed upon the cross at Calvary would reconcile those who believed. Not only was God faithful to mankind, He was faithful to His Son when He raised Jesus from the dead after His work was completed.

Because of the LORD'S great love we are not consumed, for His compassions never fail. They are new every morning; great is Your faithfulness.

Lamentations 3:22–23

Into Your hands I commit my spirit; deliver me, LORD, my faithful God.

Psalm 31:5

"The LORD is righteous in all His ways and faithful in all He does."

Psalm 145:17

The one who calls you is faithful, and he will do it.

1 Thess. 5:24 NIV

6

THE ONE WHO HEALS AND DELIVERS, MOVING IN WISDOM AND INSIGHT, MERCY AND TENDERNESS

The news about Him spread throughout all Syria; and they brought to Him all who were ill, those suffering with various diseases and pains, demoniacs, epileptics, paralytics; and He healed them all.

Matthew 4:24

The One who knows us best loves us in a way that is past our understanding. He transforms us from the inside out, knowing what needs to take place in our lives, just at the right time as we choose Him to be not only Savior but also Lord. As we turn from selfishness, He will do exceedingly, abundantly more than we could ever think or imagine through His Spirit within us.

Then a shoot will spring from the stem of Jesse, and a branch from his roots will bear fruit. The Spirit of the LORD will rest on Him, the spirit of wisdom and understanding, the spirit of counsel and strength, the spirit of knowledge and the fear of the LORD. And He will delight in the fear of the LORD, and He will not judge by what His eyes see, nor make a decision by what His ears hear; but with righteousness He will judge the poor, and decide with fairness for the afflicted of the earth...

Isaiah 11:1-4a

I shall make mention of the lovingkindness of the LORD, the praises of the LORD, according to all that the LORD has granted us, And the great goodness toward the house of Israel, Which He has granted them according to His compassion And according to the abundance of His lovingkindness.

Isaiah 63:7

7

THE ONE WHO SEES AND UNDERSTANDS, FORGIVES AND RESTORES

For His eyes are upon the ways of a man, and He sees all his steps.

Job 34:21

The vast character of the uncreated God is beyond our ability to grasp, yet in all His awesome ways, we can experience His unconditional love, His overshadowing Presence, and His gentle, comforting care. He is the keeper of His people. God's goodness leads His children to acknowledge and confess sin resulting in reconciliation and restoring relationship.

Great is our Lord and abundant in strength; His understanding is infinite.

Psalm 147:5

But Jesus was saying, "Father, forgive them; for they do not know what they are doing." And they cast lots, dividing up His garments among themselves.

Luke 23:34

The LORD is my Shepherd, I shall not want. He makes me lie down in green pastures; He leads me beside quiet waters. He restores my soul; He guides me in the paths of righteousness for His name's sake.

Psalm 23:1–3

8

HE WHO RECONCILES SLEEPS NOT

For it was the Father's good pleasure for all the fullness to dwell in Him, and through Him to reconcile all things to Himself, having made peace through the blood of His cross; through Him, I say, whether things on earth or things in heaven."

Colossians 1:19–20

The love of God has worked to bring forth a unity among men that would satisfy His heart for relational oneness. He is perfectly complete in Himself and desires to enjoy close and meaningful relationship with His creation. Genuine love gathers, gives, embraces, covers and restores.

For Christ himself has brought peace to us. He united Jews and Gentiles into one people when, in his own body on the cross, he broke down the wall of hostility that separated us. He did this by ending the system of law with

its commandments and regulations. He made peace between Jews and Gentiles by creating in himself one new people from the two groups. Together as one body, Christ reconciled both groups to God by means of his death on the cross, and our hostility toward each other was put to death.

Ephesians 2:14–16 NLT

I will lift up my eyes to the mountains; from where shall my help come? My help comes from the LORD who made heaven and earth. He will not allow your foot to slip; He who keeps you will not slumber. Behold, He who keeps Israel will neither slumber nor sleep

Psalm 121:1–4

9

THE ONE WHO KNOWS THE END FROM THE BEGINNING

eclaring the end from the beginning, and from ancient times things which have not been done, saying, 'My purpose will be established, and I will accomplish all My good pleasure.'

Isaiah 46:10

When the prophet speaks God's words years before they come to pass, we see His sovereignty in action when we know it has happened just as He said. Does your faith allow you to take God at His Word?

Then He said to me, "It is done. I am the Alpha and the Omega, the beginning and the end. I will give to the one who thirsts from the spring of the water of life without cost."

Revelation 21:6

10

HE WHO OPENS AND NO ONE CAN SHUT

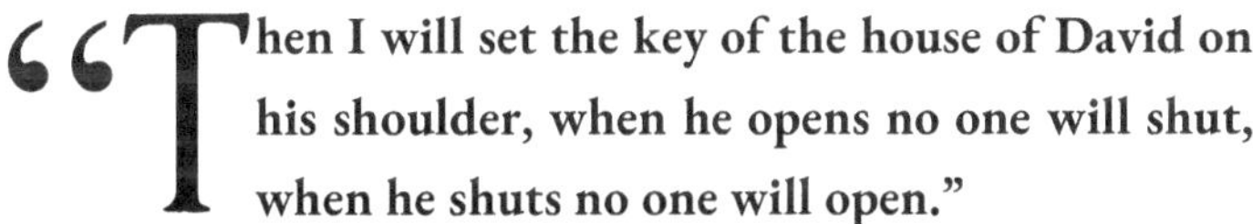

"Then I will set the key of the house of David on his shoulder, when he opens no one will shut, when he shuts no one will open."

Isaiah 22:22

When Christ walked in the authority given to Him because of His humility and obedience to the Father, there was nothing that could stand against Him. For committed believers and followers of Christ today, we have the opportunity to walk in the authority given to us by Christ. The standard is the same: humility and obedience to God's Word and devotion to fostering and maintaining a deep and uncompromising relationship with the Holy Spirit. The key of authority is given to those whose heart is committed to God. Do you walk in the authority Christ has made available to you?

And to the angel of the church in Philadelphia write: He who is holy, who is true, who has the key of David, who opens and no one will shut, and who shuts and no one opens, says this: "I know your deeds. Behold, I have put before you an open door which no one can shut, because you have a little power, and have kept My word, and have not denied My name."

Revelation 3:7

11

HE WHO INSPIRES AND CREATES, MOVES AND WAITS—NEVER TIRES

For behold, He who forms mountains and creates the wind And declares to man what are His thoughts, He who makes dawn into darkness And treads on the high places of the earth, The LORD God of hosts is His name.

Amos 4:13

It amazes me that God waits upon man; His patience is never-ending. His purpose is set, and He draws people to Himself in various and individual ways. As Creator, He knows and understands the uniqueness of each person; He is not in a hurry to wait for us to respond to His promptings. This will always amaze me. Are you aware that God often waits for your response to His Word?

For thus says the LORD, who created the heavens (He is the God who formed the earth and made it, He established it and did not create it a waste place, but formed it to be inhabited), "I am the LORD, and there is none else."

Isaiah 45:18

The LORD has looked down from heaven upon the sons of men to see if there are any who understand, who seek after God.

Psalm 14:2

All Scripture is inspired by God and profitable for teaching, for reproof, for correction, for training in righteousness; so that the man of God may be adequate, equipped for every good work.

II Timothy 3:16–17

12

FATHER, MOTHER, BROTHER, FRIEND, SAVIOR, SPOUSE, BELOVED, DESIRE OF THE NATIONS

Jesus said to her, "Stop clinging to Me, for I have not yet ascended to the Father; but go to My brethren, and say to them, I ascend to My Father and your Father, and My God and your God."

John 20:17

The Living God is the lover of the soul of mankind. His goodness comes to us in many ways to touch the deep need that is within each being. "The God who made the world and all things in it, since He is Lord of heaven and earth, does not dwell in temples made with hands; nor is He served by human hands, as though He needed anything, since He Himself gives to all people life and breath and all things." Acts 17:24–25

Whatever the need of the human soul, its source is found in Christ who is the Way and the Truth and the Life. His life is the light that shines in the darkness of our soul illuminating us within, removing fear of separation and filling each soul with peace. Our deepest need is satisfied as we experience Him in all of His fullness being released from within by His life. Have you received the deposit of His love for you today?

God created man in His own image, in the image of God He created him; male and female He created them.

Genesis 1:27

Surly I have calmed and quieted my soul; like a weaned child (resting) with his mother, my soul is like a weaned child within me (composed and freed from discontent). O Israel, hope in the LORD from this time forth and forever.

Psalm 131:2–3 AMP

For those whom He foreknew, He also predestined to become conformed to the image of His Son, so that He would be the firstborn among many brethren.

Romans 8:29

No longer do I call you slaves, for the slave does not know what his master is doing; but I have called you friends, for all things that I have heard from My Father I have made known to you.

John 15:15

But now has been revealed by the appearing of our Savior Christ Jesus who abolished death, and brought life and immortality to light through the gospel.

2 Timothy 1:10

"For your husband is your Maker, whose name is the LORD of hosts; and your Redeemer is the Holy One of Israel, who is called the God of all the earth. For the LORD has called you, like a wife forsaken and grieved in spirit, even like a wife of one's youth when she is rejected," says your God.

Isaiah 54:5–6

And after being baptized, Jesus went up immediately from the water; and behold, the heavens were opened, and he saw the Spirit of God descending as a dove, and coming upon Him, and behold, a voice out of the heavens, saying, "This is my beloved Son, in whom I am well pleased."

Matthew 3:16–17

For thus says the LORD of hosts: 'Once more (it is a little while) I will shake all nations, and they shall come to the Desire of All Nations, and I will fill this temple with glory,' says the LORD of hosts.

Haggai 2:6–7 N KJV

13

NAME ABOVE ALL NAMES; THE HIGH AND HOLY MAJESTIC ONE; EVER-PRESENT, ALL-KNOWING, ALL-POWERFUL GOD

For thus says the high and exalted One Who lives forever, whose name is Holy, I dwell on a high and holy place, and also with the contrite and lowly of spirit in order to revive the spirit of the lowly and to revive the heart of the contrite.

Isaiah 57:15

The God who is above all answers to no one; yet He humbled Himself and took upon flesh that through His supreme sacrifice, reconciled humanity and became the author of salvation for all who would believe. "The Son of Man came eating and drinking, and they say, 'Behold, a gluttonous man and a drunkard, a friend of tax collectors and sinners!' Yet wisdom is justified by her deeds." (Matthew 11:19)

Jesus put action to His words and history was changed eternally. Have you done anything in your sphere of influence that has made a significant difference in the lives of those you know?

Let this mind be in you all, which was also in Christ Jesus, who, being in the form of God, did not consider equality with God something to be grasped. But He emptied Himself, taking upon Himself the form of a servant, and was made in the likeness of men. And being found in the form of a man, He humbled Himself and became obedient to death, even death on a cross. Therefore God highly exalted Him and gave Him the name which is above every name, that at the name of Jesus every knee should bow, of those in heaven and on earth and under the earth, and every tongue should confess that Jesus Christ is Lord, to the glory of God the Father.

Philippians 2:5–11

I will worship toward Your holy temple, and praise Your name for Your lovingkindness and for Your truth; for You have exalted Your word above all Your name.

Psalm 138:2 MEV

He counts the number of the stars; He calls them all by their names.

Psalm 147:4

Then the LORD answered Job out of the whirlwind and said:

"Prepare yourself now like a man; I will question you, and you will answer Me. Will you indeed annul My judgment? Will you condemn Me, that you may be righteous? Have you an arm like God? Or can you thunder with a voice like Him? Adorn yourself now with majesty and excellence, and array yourself with glory and beauty. Loose the rage of your wrath, and look on every one who is proud and abase him; look on every one who is proud and bring him low, and tread down the wicked in their place. Hide them in the dust together, and imprison them in the hidden place of the grave. Then I will also confess to you that your own right hand can save you."

Job 40:6–14

For all have sinned and come short of the glory of God.

Romans 3:23

You are worthy, O Lord, to receive glory and honor and power; for You have created all things, and by Your will they exist and were created.

Revelation 4:11

Then I looked, and I heard around the throne and the living creatures and the elders the voices of many angels, numbering ten thousand times ten thousand, and thousands of thousands, saying with a loud voice: Worthy is the Lamb who was slain, to receive power and riches and wisdom and strength and honor and glory and blessing.

Revelation 5:11

Look, I am coming soon! My reward is with Me to give to each one according to his work. I am the Alpha and the Omega, the Beginning and the End, the First and the Last.

Revelation 22:12 MEV

14

THE PERFECT ONE, LACKING NOTHING, POSSESSOR AND SUSTAINER OF ALL THINGS

As for God, His way is perfect; the word of the LORD is proven; He is a shield for all who take refuge in Him.

2 Samuel 22:31 MEV

Those who trust in God can rest in His eternal care. He is perfect and all that He does reflects His divine nature. God has initiated all life that exists and He sustains His created order. Nothing is hidden from His sight and He causes the sun to shine on the just and the unjust alike.

The Rock! His work is perfect; For all His ways are just;

A God of faithfulness and without injustice, Righteous and upright is He.

Deuteronomy 32:4

The God who made the world and all things in it, since He is Lord of heaven and earth, does not dwell in temples made with hands; nor is He served by human hands, as though He needed anything, since He Himself gives to all people life and breath and all things.

Acts 17:24–25

The earth is the LORD'S, and all it contains, the world, and those who dwell in it.

Psalm 24:1

You open Your hand and satisfy the desire of every living thing.

Psalm 145:16

But now ask the beasts, and let them teach you; And the birds of the heavens, and let them tell you. Or speak to the earth, and let it teach you; And let the fish of the sea declare to you. Who among all these does not know That the hand of the LORD has done this, In whose hand is the life of every living thing, And the breath of all mankind?

Job 12:7–10

For just as the Father has life in Himself, even so He gave to the Son also to have life in Himself.

John 5:26

This is the will of Him who sent Me, that of all that He has given Me I lose nothing, but raise it up on the last day.

John 6:39

15

THE FRUITFUL ONE, THE VINE

I am the true vine, and My Father is the vinedresser. Abide in Me, and I in you. As the branch cannot bear fruit of itself unless it abides in the vine, so neither can you unless you abide in Me. I am the vine, you are the branches; he who abides in Me and I in him, he bears much fruit, for apart from me you can do nothing.

John 15:1,4–5

As we develop an on-going relationship with the risen Christ in the Word of God and prayer, we are assured by Him that we will bring forth much fruit. Fruitfulness is an earmark of God's kingdom, which will affect the sphere of our influence bringing multiple blessing. All God did was to initiate and foster life, and as His followers we have an opportunity to help release His goodness to humanity. How can you be a blessing to someone today?

Jesus answered them, "The hour has come for the Son of Man to be glorified. Truly, truly I say to you, unless a grain of wheat falls into the ground and dies, it remains alone. But if it dies, it bears much fruit. He who loves his life will lose it. And he who hates his life in this world will keep it for eternal life. If anyone serves Me, he must follow Me. Where I am, there will My servant be also. If anyone serves Me, the Father will honor him.

John 12:23–26 MEV

16

THE WATER OF LIFE, HE WHO CLEANSES

And he showed me a river of the water of life, clear as crystal, coming from the throne of God and of the Lamb, in the middle of its street. And on either side of the river was the tree of life, bearing twelve kinds of fruit, yielding its fruit every month; and the leaves of the tree were for the healing of the nations.

Revelation 22:1–2

The work of sanctification, being set apart by God for God, is an on-going work of His Spirit. Water is used to clean dirt off and bring renewal. God's written Word and Christ, the living Word, work to cleanse a person from the defilement sin has caused. By faith we are separated to God, and by faith we will continually be changed from within as our mind is renewed and our decisions and choices show the effect of God's Spirit. We no longer have to fear God, for He has given us a nature just like His. Even though we will be changing as we grow in Christ, we can now draw close to God and enjoy Him without guilt and shame. Are you able to see yourself completely clean and new by God's design?

Therefore, brethren, since we have confidence to enter the holy place by the blood of Jesus, by a new and living way which He inaugurated for us through the veil, that is, His flesh, and since we have a great priest over the house of God, let us draw near with a sincere heart in full assurance of faith, having our hearts sprinkled clean from an evil conscience and our bodies washed with pure water.

Hebrews 10:19–22

Such were some of you; but you were washed, but you were sanctified, but you were justified in the name of the Lord Jesus Christ and in the Spirit of our God.

1 Corinthians 6:11

Then He said to me, "It is done. I am the Alpha and the Omega, the beginning and the end. I will give to the one who thirsts from the spring of the water of life without cost."

Revelation 21:6

The Spirit and the bride say, "Come." Let him who hears say, "Come." Let him who is thirsty come; let him who wishes take the water of life without cost.

Revelation 22:17

17

THE BREAD OF LIFE, HE WHO SATISFIES

Then Jesus said, "Truly, truly I say to you, Moses did not give you the bread from heaven, but My Father gives you the true bread from heaven." "For the bread of God is He who comes down from heaven and gives life to the world." "I am the bread of life. Whoever comes to Me shall never hunger, and whoever believes in Me shall never thirst." "I am the living bread which came down from heaven. If anyone eats of this bread, he will live forever. The bread which I shall give for the life of the world is My flesh." "This is the bread which came down from heaven, not as your fathers ate manna and died. He who eats this bread will live forever."

John 6:32,33,35, 51,58 MEV

Bread is common to all cultures and it is food that satisfies. Jesus gave His flesh and blood as a sacrifice on the cross as the payment for sin. By faith in Christ's finished work, all who believe can be united to Him, the true source of life that will last forever. The essence of Christ, when received, brings a satisfaction deep within our being that no earthly substitute can fulfill. Just as bread nourishes our bodies, Christ is the nourishment we need to grow spiritually. The Spirit God brings His life into us to strengthen us within. The resurrected life of Jesus affects us from the inside out. Evidence of His life will manifest in our new way of thinking, speaking, and acting. A heavenly perspective will replace the old way of living. Change happens within and is witnessed through the new character of our heart, mind, and actions. Jesus, the Bread of Life, is seen again in our world through our life.

Since you have in obedience to the truth purified your souls for a sincere love of the brethren, fervently love one another from the heart, for you have been born again not of seed which is perishable but imperishable, that is, through the living and enduring word of God.

1 Peter 1:22–23

18

THE LIGHT OF THE WORLD; OUR TEACHER

Then Jesus again spoke to them, saying, "I am the Light of the world; he who follows Me will not walk in the darkness, but will have the Light of life."

John 8:12

When we are born from above and the light of Christ's life enlightens us, Heaven has come down. Eternal light has been turned on and we can see from a new perspective. The Light of Heaven is teaching us that the life coming from Christ enlightens us to see the darkness of our sin nature. Our Teacher shows us this reality so that we can choose to turn away from the darkness of sin to the new way of life in Christ.

But the Helper, the Holy Spirit, whom the Father will send in My name, He will teach you all things, and bring to your remembrance all that I said to you.

John 14:26

You are the light of the world. A city set on a hill cannot be hidden; nor does anyone light a lamp and put it under a basket, but on the lampstand, and it gives light to all who are in the house. Let your light shine before men in such a way that they may see your good works, and glorify your Father who is in heaven.

Matthew 5:14–16

For You will light my lamp; The Lord my God illumines my darkness.

Psalm 18:28

For God, who said, "Light shall shine out of darkness," is the One who has shone in our hearts to give the Light of the knowledge of the glory of God in the face of Christ.

2 Corinthians 4:6

19

THE UNSEEN, EVER-PRESENT ONE WHO FILLS THE EARTH WITH GOODNESS

All honor and glory to God forever and ever! He is the eternal King, the unseen one who never dies; he alone is God. Amen.

1 Timothy 1:17 NLT

The unseen God who spoke all things into existence with a word continues to work in the affairs of humanity. Although we cannot see Him with our natural eyes, we do see His creativity and wonders in creation. Who could put the galaxy in its place, set the stars above and cause the planets, sun and moon to function without the cooperation or interference of man? Who keeps the oceans in place?

Believing in the triune God makes the Father real as we see Jesus and the works He manifested and listen to the words He spoke concerning God and His Kingdom. By faith we believe God was in Jesus doing His work, and by faith we trust in the fullness of redemption through Christ's sacrifice on the cross.

God came to Earth as the Son of Man to make Himself known, not only to all of humanity but to each person individually. Jesus is not only the Savior of the world, but He becomes the personal Savior of all who put their faith in Him.

God's goodness, mercy and grace came to show His unconditional love through the life of His Son. The One who is all-knowing and all-powerful is also present at all times everywhere. He is Almighty God.

Jesus said to him, "Have I been so long with you, and yet you have not come to know Me, Philip? He who has seen Me has seen the Father; how do you say, 'Show us the Father"?

John 14:9

For the eyes of the LORD search the whole earth in order to strengthen those whose hearts are fully committed to him.

11 Chronicles 16:9 NLT

He loves righteousness and justice; The earth is full of the goodness of the LORD.

Psalm 33:5 NKJV

20

THE GENTLE ONE MOVING IN COMPASSION

Through the LORD'S mercies we are not consumed, Because His compassions fail not. They are new every morning;

Great is Your faithfulness.

Lamentations 3:22–23 NKJV

To say that we know the Lord and yet have never experienced Him moving in mercy and compassion over us is only head-knowledge. Out of God's heart flows love, joy, peace, patience, kindness, goodness, faithfulness, gentleness, and self-control. The essence of who He is will be evident as we walk in humility and meekness. To love as God loves can only flow from the heart that has been yielded and receptive to Him. Liberty is natural to those who are confident of their Father's heart and love as He loves.

You have also given me the shield of Your salvation; Your gentleness has made me great.

2 Samuel 22:36 NKJV

So He said, "Go forth and stand on the mountain before the LORD." And behold, the LORD was passing by! And a strong wind was rending the mountains and breaking in pieces the rocks before the LORD; but the LORD was not in the wind. And after the wind an earthquake, but the LORD was not in the earthquake. After the earthquake a fire, but the LORD was not in the fire; and after the fire a sound of a gentle blowing.

1 Kings 19:11–12

The LORD is gracious and full of compassion, Slow to anger and great in mercy.

Psalm 145:8 NKJV

And Jesus, when He came out, saw a great multitude and was moved with compassion for them, because they were like sheep not having a shepherd. So He began to teach them many things.

Mark 6:34 NKJV

21

THE JEALOUS LOVER, PASSIONATE AND PROTECTIVE

For you shall worship no other god, for the LORD, whose name is Jealous, is a jealous God...

Exodus 34:14

The jealousy of the LORD our God is a passionate and protective emotion that flows from the heart of His pure essence, which is holy, unconditional love. There is no defilement in God; therefore, the jealousy He speaks of can never wound or abuse. Love that is perfect will work to protect us from everything that is not coming to us from love.

Christ's sacrificial death upon the cross is referred to as the Passion. Extravagant love expressed in action is the jealous, passionate manifestation of His body willingly nailed to the cross; His blood the payment for our sin.

So watch yourselves, lest you forget the covenant of the LORD your God, which He made with you, and make for yourselves a graven image in the form of anything against which the LORD your God has commanded you. For the LORD your God is a consuming fire, a jealous God.

Deuteronomy 4:23–24

Then the word of the LORD of hosts came, saying, "Thus says the LORD of hosts, 'I am exceedingly jealous for Zion, yes, with great wrath I am jealous for her.'"

Zechariah 8:1–2

22

THE HOLY ONE FILLED WITH ALL KNOWLEDGE

O LORD, You have searched me and known me. You know my sitting down and my rising up; You understand my thought afar off. You comprehend my path and my lying down And are acquainted with all my ways. For there is not a word on my tongue, But behold, O LORD, You know it altogether.

You have hedged me behind and before And laid Your hand upon me. Such knowledge is too wonderful for me; It is high, I cannot attain it. Where can I go from Your Spirit? Or where can I flee from Your presence? If I ascend into heaven, You are there; If I make my bed in hell, behold, You are there. If I take the wings of the morning, And dwell in the uttermost parts of the sea, Even there Your hand shall lead me, And Your right hand shall hold me.

If I say, "Surely the darkness shall fall on me," Even the night shall be light about me; Indeed, the darkness shall not hide from You, But the night shines as the day; The darkness and the light are both alike to You. [13] For You formed my inward parts; You covered me in my mother's womb. I will praise You, for I am fearfully and wonderfully made; Marvelous are Your works, And that my soul knows very well.

My frame was not hidden from You, When I was made in secret, And skillfully wrought in the lowest parts of the earth. Your eyes saw my substance, being yet unformed. And in Your book they all were written, The days fashioned for me, When as yet there were none of them.

Psalm 139:1–16 NKJV

The All-Knowing God, who with a word spoke the universe into existence, He is the Holy God. There is not another like Him and we will never fully know or understand Him. He says that His ways are not our ways. His ways are superior, yet He draws us to Himself so that He may reveal Himself to us so that we may know His reality and experience who He is. God's intention is that we might live in relationship with Him; that we may grow in understanding of God the Father, Christ Jesus the Son, and God the Holy Spirit, each a different expression of the heart and mind of God revealed through their activity in our lives.

Remember the former things long past, For I am God, and there is no other; I am God, and there is no one like Me, Declaring the end from the beginning, And from ancient times things which have not been done, Saying, "My purpose will be established, And I will accomplish all My good pleasure."

Isaiah 46:9–10

When I consider Your heavens, the work of Your fingers, The moon and the stars, which You have ordained; What is man that You take thought of him, And the son of man that You care for him?

Psalm 8:3–4

23

THE DAY-STAR WHO GOES BEFORE HIS PEOPLE, MAKING THE CROOKED STRAIGHT AND LEVELING EVERY EXALTED PLACE

So we have the prophetic word made more sure, to which you do well to pay attention as to a lamp shining in a dark place, until the day dawns and the morning star arises in your hearts.

2 Peter 1:19–20

God has always gone before His people and prepared a way for them; whether by the word of prophecy spoken centuries before the fulfillment or His providential hand moving in the affairs of people to have them at the right place at the right time to meet the right person. God-Creator-Father is working secretly behind the scenes to bring about His purposes in the earth. He is sovereign and there is no one like Him.

The voice of him that crieth in the wilderness, Prepare ye the way of the LORD, make straight in the desert a highway for our God. Every valley shall be exalted, and every mountain and hill shall be made low: and the crooked shall be made straight, and the rough places plain: And the glory of the LORD shall be revealed, and all flesh shall see it together: for the mouth of the LORD hath spoken it.

Isaiah 40:3–5 KJV

And the LORD went before them by day in a pillar of cloud to lead the way, and by night in a pillar of fire to give them light, so as to go by day and night. He did not take away the pillar of cloud by day or the pillar of fire by night from before the people.

Exodus 13:21–22 NKJV

But you will not go out in haste, Nor will you go as fugitives; For the LORD will go before you, And the God of Israel will be your rear guard.

Isaiah 52:12

Now in those days John the Baptist came, preaching in the wilderness of Judea, saying, "Repent, for the kingdom of heaven is at hand." For this is the one referred to by Isaiah the prophet when he said, "The voice of one crying in the wilderness, 'Make ready the way of the LORD, make His paths straight!'"

Matthew 3:1–3

24

HE WHO SEES JUDGES NOT AND YET HIS JUDGEMENT IS IN THE EARTH

And if anyone hears My sayings, and does not keep them, I do not judge him; for I did not come to judge the world, but to save the world. He who rejects Me, and does not receive My sayings, has one who judges him; the word I spoke is what will judge him at the last day.

John 12:47–48

You have heard it said, "men are their own worst enemies," and I believe this can be true. We make wrong choices and then have to deal with the consequences. We reap what we sow, and oftentimes that is contrary to what God would have for us. If we choose irresponsible behavior and bad things happen because of that choice, then it is our own fault. Over the years, I have heard people say they would to do a certain thing or go to a particular function; yet they end up doing what they really want to do instead of what they initially said. God sees us and hears us and watches what we do. His desire is not judgement but life. Jesus said that He did not come to judge the world but to save it. People bring judgement upon themselves by what they do or fail to do. The things that are done reveal the true desire of our heart.

Then she called the name of the LORD who spoke to her, "Thou art a God who sees," for she said, "Have I even remained alive here after seeing Him?"

Genesis 16:13

You show lovingkindness to thousands, and repay the iniquity of the fathers into the bosom of their children after them—the Great, the Mighty God, whose name is the LORD of hosts. You are great in counsel and mighty in work, for Your eyes are open to all the ways of the sons of men, to give everyone according to his ways and according to the fruit of his doings.

Jeremiah 32:18–19 NKJV

Do not be deceived, God is not mocked; for whatever a man sows, that he will also reap. For he who sows to his flesh will of the flesh reap corruption, but he who sows to the Spirit will of the Spirit reap everlasting life.

Galatians 6:7–8 NKJV

25

THE EVER-FLOWING STREAM OF LIFE, NOURISHING THE EARTH

There is a river whose streams make glad the city of God, The holy dwelling places of the Most-High.

Psalm 46:4

To God, the creator of all that exists, His standard is high, higher than ours. He watches over all the works of His hands and satisfies the desire of every living thing. He knows and prepares ahead for the needs of those who live upon the earth and especially for those who believe in Him and pray to Him in faith.

O LORD, how many are Your works! In wisdom You have made them all; The earth is full of Your possessions. There is the sea, great and broad, In which are swarms without number, Animals both small and great. There the ships move along, And Leviathan, which You have formed to sport in it. They all wait for You to give them their food

in due season. You give to them, they gather it up; You open Your hand, they are satisfied with good.

Psalms 104:24–28

For your Father knows the things you have need of before you ask Him. In this manner, therefore pray: Our Father in heaven, Hallowed by Your name. Your kingdom come. Your will be done on earth as it is in heaven. Give us this day our daily bread.

Matthew 6:8–11

You have heard that it was said, 'You shall love your neighbor and hate your enemy.' But I say to you, love your enemies and pray for those who persecute you, so that you may be sons of your Father who is in heaven; for He causes His sun to rise on the evil and the good, and sends rain on the righteous and the unrighteous.

Matthew 5:43–45

26

THE ONE WHO SHEPHERDS, GUIDES AND CORRECTS

I am the good shepherd; the good shepherd lays down His life for the sheep.

John 10:11

Jesus Christ has already paid the price required by our Holy God to be the One who is worthy of the title The Good Shepherd. By His blood He purchased us back from Satan, and we are God's children and those who follow the Shepherd wherever He leads. Our Father sends His Holy Spirit to guide us out of darkness and into the light of His truth. He has secured our place as God's adopted children and a place in God's kingdom that we may fulfill the works He has planned for us to accomplish in Christ.

Yahweh is my best friend and my shepherd. I always have more than enough. He offers a resting place for me in his luxurious love. His tracks take me to an oasis of peace near the quiet brook of bliss. That's where he restores and revives my life. He opens before me the right path and leads me along in his footsteps of righteousness so that I can bring honor to his name. Even when your path takes me through the valley of deepest darkness, fear will never conquer me, for you already have! Your authority is my strength and my peace. The comfort of your love takes away my fear. I'll never be lonely, for you are near. You become my delicious feast even when my enemies dare to fight. You anoint me with the fragrance of your Holy Spirit; you give me all I can drink of you until my cup overflows. So why would I fear the future? Only goodness and tender love pursue me all the days of my life. Then afterward, when my life is through, I'll return to your glorious presence to be forever with you!

Psalm 23 TPT

For such is God, our God forever and ever; He will guide us until death.

Psalm 48:14

But when He, the Spirit of truth comes, He will guide you into all the truth; for He will not speak on His own initiative, but whatever He hears, He will speak, and He will disclose to you what is to come.

John 16:13

I will be a father to him, and he will be a son to Me; when he commits iniquity, I will correct him with the rod of men and the strokes of the sons of men.

2 Samuel 7:14

27

THE BEAUTIFUL RADIANT ONE WHO FILLS THE EARTH WITH SONG, COLOR AND BEAUTY

And He was transfigured before them; and His face shone like the sun, and His garments became as white as light.

Matthew 17:2

Isaiah, prophetically describing the suffering Messiah in the 53rd chapter, said that there was no stately form that would make us want to look upon Him or be attracted to Him, yet David said in Psalm 27 that he wanted to dwell in the house of the LORD all the days of his life to behold the beauty (or delightfulness) of his God.

This Creator-God who paints our world with breathtaking sunsets causes the birds to sing unending love songs, reveals the unfolding beauty of a budding rose and the delicate wonder of each individual petal of every flower, radiates the beauty and wonder of life that issues from His essence. The heart of God expressed in the life of His Son is the expression of the Holy One who lives in unapproachable light.

And in His right hand He held seven stars; and out of His mouth came a sharp two-edged sword; and His face was like the sun shining in its strength.

Revelation 1:16

Then Moses and the sons of Israel sang this song to the LORD, and said, "I will sing to the LORD, for He is highly exalted; the horse and its rider He has hurled into the sea. The LORD is my strength and song, and He has become my salvation. This is my God and I will praise Him; My father's God, and I will extol Him."

Exodus 15:1–2

Sing to the LORD, all the earth; proclaim the good news of His salvation from day to day.

1 Chronicles 16:23

O afflicted one, storm-tossed, and not comforted, Behold, I will set your stones in antimony, and your foundations I will lay in sapphires, moreover, I will make your battlements of rubies, and your gates of crystal, and your entire wall of precious stones.

Isaiah 54:11–12

He has made everything beautiful in its time.

Ecclesiastes 3:11a

28

THE RELENTLESS LOVER WHO PURSUES AND OVERCOMES

The Lord appeared to him from afar, saying, "I have loved you with an everlasting love; Therefore I have drawn you with loving kindness. Again I will build you and you will be rebuilt, O virgin of Israel!"

Jeremiah 31:3–4

The lover of man's soul completely abandoned Himself to the will of God to pay the price for sin that He might have a bride who would choose Him because of love. He who obeyed unto death, overcoming death and the grave, would win the heart of all who see Him in spirit and in truth. He was tempted just as we are, yet He never fell short of God's glorious standard; and His devotion was so pure that He never grieved His Father's heart. A holy sacrifice was required to purchase back humanity from the depravity of sin's power, and Jesus overcame every form of temptation that is common to man. He set the standard of everyone who is born from above.

So He told them this parable, saying, "What man among you, if he has a hundred sheep and has lost one of them, does not leave the ninety-nine in the open pasture and go after the one which is lost until he finds it?"

Luke 15:3–4

For we do not have a high priest who cannot sympathize with our weaknesses, but One who has been tempted in all things as we are, yet without sin.

Hebrews 4:15

The LORD will go forth like a warrior, He will arouse His zeal like a man of war. He will utter a shout, yes, He will raise a war cry. He will prevail against His enemies.

Isaiah 42:13

I am the good shepherd; the good shepherd lays down His life for the sheep.

John 10:11

29

HE WHO FILLS MY MOUTH WITH GOOD THINGS AND WHOSE STRENGTH NEVER FAILS

My heart overflows with a good theme; I address my verses to the King; My tongue is the pen of a ready writer. I will cause Your name to be remembered in all generations; therefore, the peoples will give You thanks forever and ever."

Psalm 45:1, 17

All praise, glory and honor to God alone who has given new life, new hope, a new path, new vision, and new purpose. His joy is our strength for He has obtained victory over every obstacle and every opposing way. He has made us united to the source of strength that comes from Christ's overcoming life, and praise flows from a heart of gratitude and devotion.

Willingly I will sacrifice to You; I will give thanks to Your name, O LORD, for it is good.

Psalm 54:6

He delivers me from my enemies; surely You lift me above those who rise up against me; You rescue me from the violent man. Therefore, I will give thanks to You among the nations, O LORD, and I will sing praises to Your name.

Psalm 18:48–49

I will give thanks to the LORD with all my heart; I will tell of all Your wonders.

Psalm 9:1

And He has said to me, "My grace is sufficient for you, for power is perfected in weakness. Most gladly, therefore, I will rather boast about my weaknesses, so that the power of Christ may dwell in me."

2 Corinthians 12:9

Blessed be the LORD, my rock, who trains my hands for war, and my fingers for battle; My lovingkindness and my fortress, my stronghold and my deliverer, my shield and He in whom I take refuge, Who subdues my people under me.

Psalm 144:1–2

Behold, God is my salvation, I will trust and not be afraid; For the LORD GOD is my strength and song, and He has become my salvation.

Isaiah 12:1

30

THE LIGHT IN THE DARKNESS, THE FLAME THAT CANNOT BE EXTINGUISHED

Then God said, "Let there be lights in the expanse of the heavens to separate the day from the night, and let them be for signs and for seasons and for days and years; and let them be for lights in the expanse of the heavens to give light on the earth"; and it was so. God made the two great lights, the greater light to govern the day, and the lesser light to govern the night; He made the stars also. God placed them in the expanse of the heavens to give light on the earth, and to govern the day and the night, and to separate the light from the darkness; and God saw that it was good."

Genesis 1:14–18

The flame of eternal covenant love burns in the heart of an awakened soul, and no one can quench it. Those who have been rescued from darkness become carriers and witnesses of the light of God's pursuit of them. The unconditional love of God for humanity displayed in the life of Christ produces a passionate heart with a purpose that will not fail. Increasing divine light releases within the grace, which enables us to overcome every dark plan perpetuated against truth. Love of God binds heart and purpose to reveal the Christ who is the Light of the world; who also is the way and the truth and the life. Christ and those whose hearts burn with unquenchable love and devotion become united with one purpose, to release the light of Jesus' life that no darkness can overcome.

Now Moses was keeping the flock of his father-in-law, Jethro, the priest of Midian, and he led his flock to the west side of the wilderness and came to Horeb, the mountain of God. And the angel of the LORD appeared to him in a flame of fire out of the midst of a bush. He looked, and behold, the bush was burning, yet it was not consumed."

Exodus 3:1–3 ESV

They said to one another, "Were not our hearts burning within us while He was speaking to us on the road, while He was explaining the Scriptures to us?"

Luke 24:32

And there appeared to them tongues as of fire distributing themselves, and they rested on each one of them.

Acts 2:3

But get up and stand on your feet; for this purpose I have appeared to you, to appoint you a minister and a witness not only to the things which you have seen, but also to the things in which I will appear to you; rescuing you from the Jewish people and from the Gentiles, to whom I am sending you, to open their eyes so that they may turn from darkness to light and from the dominion of Satan to God, that they may receive forgiveness of sins and an inheritance among those who have been sanctified by faith in Me.

Acts 26:16–18

And I heard a loud voice in heaven, saying, "Now the salvation, and the power, and the kingdom of our God and the authority of His Christ have come, for the accuser of our brethren has been thrown down, who accuses them before our God day and night. And they overcame him because of the blood of the Lamb and because of the word of their testimony, and they did not love their life even to death.

Revelation 12:10–11

31

THE FATHER OF THE PRODIGAL; LOVER OF THE HARLOT; HUSBAND TO THE WIDOW AND FATHER OF THE ORPHAN

Father of the Prodigal

So he went and hired himself out to one of the citizens of that country, and he sent him into his fields to feed swine. And he would have gladly filled his stomach with the pods that the swine were eating, and no one was giving anything to him. But when he came to his senses, he said, 'How many of my father's hired men have more than enough bread, but I am dying here with hunger!' I will get up and go to my father, and will say to him, "Father, I have sinned against heaven, and in your sight; I am no longer worthy to be called your son; make me as one of your hired men."' So he got up and came to his father. But while he was still a long way off, his father saw him and felt compassion for him, and ran and embraced him and kissed him. And the son said to him, 'Father, I have sinned against heaven and in your sight; I am no longer worthy to be called your son.' But the father said to his slaves, 'Quickly bring out the best robe and put it on him, and put a ring on his hand and sandals on his feet; and bring the fattened calf, kill it, and let us eat and celebrate; for this son of mine was dead and has come to life again; he was lost and has been found.' And they began to celebrate."

Luke 15:15–24

Lover of the Harlot

Listen to the word of the LORD, O sons of Israel, For the LORD has a case against the inhabitants of the land, Because there is no faithfulness or kindness or knowledge of God in the land. There is swearing, deception, murder, stealing and adultery. They employ violence, so that bloodshed follows bloodshed.

Hosea 4:1–2

For my people are determined to desert me. They call me the Most-High, but they don't truly honor me. Oh, how can I give you up, Israel? How can I let you go? How can I destroy you like Admah or demolish you like Zeboiim? My heart is torn within me, and my compassion overflows. No, I will not unleash my fierce anger. I will not completely destroy Israel, for I am God and not a mere mortal. I am the Holy One living among you, and I will not come to destroy.

Hosea 11:7–9 NLT

<u>Husband to the Widow- Father of the Orphan</u>

"Fear not, for you will not be put to shame; Neither feel humiliated, for you will not be disgraced; but you will forget the shame of your youth, And the reproach of your widowhood you will remember no more. For your husband is your Maker, Whose name is the LORD of hosts; And your Redeemer is the Holy One of Israel, Who is called the God of all the earth."

Isaiah 54:4–5

"A father of the fatherless, a defender of widows, is God in His holy habitation. God sets the solitary in families; He brings out those who are bound into prosperity; but the rebellious dwell in a dry land."

Psalm 68:5–6 NKJV

For the LORD your God is God of gods and Lord of lords, the great God, mighty and awesome, who shows no partiality nor takes a bribe. He administers justice for the fatherless and the widow, and loves the stranger, giving him food and clothing."

Deuteronomy 10:17–18 NKJV

The Father longs to be in relationship with those who have gone their own way. His heart is not complete until they return home. He waits for the perfect time to convict and to draw them to Himself being ready to accept them with open arms. The Father's forgiveness removes the shame and He covers the new believer with His righteousness. When hearts are divided and not fully committed to covenant love, God tries to turn His wayward sons and daughters around. He is relentless in His pursuit of us, yet never forces His way upon anyone. Love must be chosen by the heart who sees God for who He is and who knows their desperate state apart from His love, care and provision. He waits for people to see His grace and goodness and to choose Him. God also has provision for all the needy, especially those who are alone without family of their own. He draws them to Himself and releases care for them in many ways, showing they are not forsaken or abandoned but loved and cherished.

32

THE HEAD OF THE BODY, THE PILLAR OF STRENGTH; OUR REFUGE AND STRONG TOWER

He is also head of the body, the church; and He is the beginning, the firstborn from the dead, so that He Himself will come to have first place in everything.

Colossians 1:18

If someone severed my head from my body, that would be the end of my life. God has always been the life of His creation. The first breath of a newborn baby begins as he or she emerges from the womb. The breath of God fills every human being as He is the author and sustainer of life.

Sin initiates the great divide. Christ has redeemed and reconciled humanity back to the source of life He intended for them. United to Christ by faith we are connected to God the Father who cares for our deepest needs and desires. As people yield to the headship of Christ, the Holy Spirit will transform them to become the image of the invisible God on Earth—Christ with us, the hope of the glory of God in human flesh making Himself known through our personality.

For just as we have many members in one body and all the members do not have the same function, so we who are many, are one body in Christ, and individually members one of another.

Romans 12:4-5

The LORD is their strength, And He is a saving defense to His anointed.

Psalm 28:8

Finally, be strong in the Lord and in the strength of His might.

Ephesians 6:10

When you pass through the waters, I will be with you; And through the rivers, they will not overflow you. When you walk through the fire, you will not be scorched, Nor will the flame burn you.

Isaiah 43:2

For in the day of trouble He will conceal me in His tabernacle; In the secret place of His tent He will hide me; He will lift me up on a rock.

Psalms 27:5

33

THE DEFENSE AGAINST OUR ENEMIES, OUR ADVOCATE

And they overcame him because of the blood of the Lamb and because of the word of their testimony, and they did not love their life even when faced with death.

Rev. 12:11

The testimony of those who live with and by God's Spirit is a defense against any enemy. In the Book of Acts, when Peter was brought before his accusers, he would always ask to speak to the people. He expounded on his experience of how God had sent an angel to rescue him while he was chained between two guards. Peter thought he was dreaming, but when the angel had safely taken him out of jail and to the door of the city, he came to his senses and said, "Now I know for sure that the Lord has sent forth His angel and rescued me from the hand of Herod and from all that the Jewish people were expecting." (Acts 12:5–11)

We are never alone or separated from the God Who dwells within. When we sin and repent, Jesus' blood speaks on our behalf before God's throne, and we are forgiven and not condemned. When we need wisdom for a particular situation, we need only ask in faith, and it will be given to us. If we must make a defense to anyone concerning our faith, the Holy Spirit will give us the words needed at that very moment. With God, each believer is a conqueror through the resurrected Christ.

Oh that My people would listen to Me, that Israel would walk in My ways! I would quickly subdue their enemies and turn My hand against their adversaries.

Psalm 81:13–14

Contend, O LORD with those who contend with me; Fight against those who fight against me.

Psalm 35:1

You are my hiding place; You preserve me from trouble; You surround me with songs of deliverance.

Psalm 32:7

My little children, I am writing these things to you so that you may not sin. And if anyone sins, we have an Advocate (*Greek, one called alongside to help*) with the Father, Jesus Christ the righteous; and He Himself is the propitiation (*payment in full*) for our sins; and not for ours only, but also for those of the whole world.

1 John 2:1–2 (Italics mine)

34

HE WHO JUSTIFIES

He who was delivered up because of our transgressions, and was raised because of our justification. Therefore having been justified by faith, we have peace with God through our Lord Jesus Christ.

Romans 4:25, 5:1

Having faith in Jesus' work on the cross justifies us in the sight of God our Father. There is nothing an individual can do to free themselves from the debt of sinfulness. The nature of man cannot be transformed by personal effort. Faith in Christ's substitutional death clears us from guilt and condemnation when we accept His finished work. The path of living a righteous life begins by choosing to think the way God thinks as we receive the words of His mind and are united with the heart that forgives.

The new life in Christ enables us to overcome every temptation of the sinful, carnal nature that would lead us to walk independent of God. Living life in humble submission to the

Holy Spirit will enable a person to grow into maturity and Christ-likeness. This is the goal of Christianity.

But God demonstrated His own love toward us, in that while we were yet sinners, Christ died for us. Much more then, having now been justified by His blood, we shall be saved from the wrath of God through Him. For if while we were enemies, we were reconciled to God through the death of His Son, much more, having been reconciled, we shall be saved by His life.

Romans 5:8–10

For whom He foreknew, He also predestined to become conformed to the image of His Son, that He might be the first-born among many brethren; and whom He predestined, these He also called; and whom He called, these He also justified; and whom He justified, these He also glorified.

Romans 8:29–30

35

HE WHO GLORIFIES AND CROWNS HIS PEOPLE WITH LOVING-KINDNESS AND MERCY

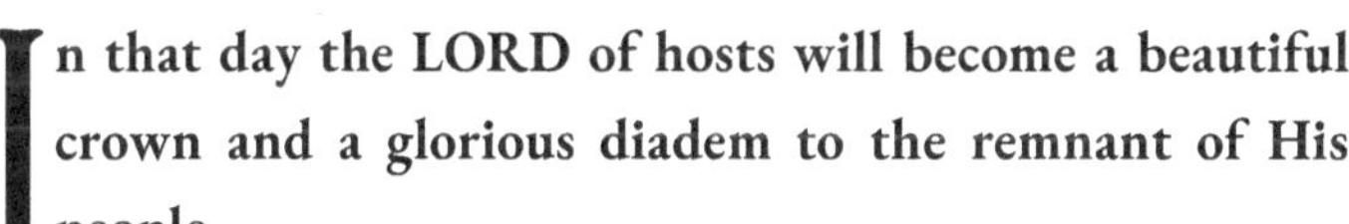

In that day the **LORD** of hosts will become a beautiful crown and a glorious diadem to the remnant of His people...

Isaiah 28:5

The Word is clear, 'no good thing will He withhold from those who walk uprightly before Him' (Psalm 84:11), including allowing us to share in His glory. From the top of our heads to the soles of our feet, God's good and perfect gifts are bestowed upon His children. Our bodies are a masterpiece of His amazing creative power. We might ask ourselves, "Why would God want to share His glory with me?" God chooses to give because of loving generosity. He is unselfish because we are the object of His love. Father God is perfect holiness and unending in mercy, releasing His Presence to those who are loyal to Jesus with their whole heart.

Who redeems your life from the pit, Who crowns you with lovingkindness and compassion.

Psalm 103:4

Those who accept my commandments and obey them are the ones who love me. And because they love me, my Father will love them. And I will love them and reveal myself to each of them.

John 14:21 NLT

The glory which You have given Me I have given to them, that they may be one, just as We are one.

John 17:22

To Him who led His people through the wilderness, For His lovingkindness is everlasting...

Psalm 136:16

Surely goodness and mercy shall follow me all the days of my life; and I will dwell in the house of the LORD forever.

Psalm 23:6 KJV

36

HE WHO EMPTIES AND HE WHO FILLS, THE ETERNAL ONE

Have this attitude in yourselves which was also in Christ Jesus, who, although He existed in the form of God, did not regard equality with God a thing to be grasped, but emptied Himself, taking the form of a bond-servant, and being made in the likeness of men.

Philippians 2:5–7

Jesus was our example. He showed us the love of God by living a sacrificial life. He laid aside His divinity and humbled Himself in becoming a servant. As we follow His example, we are filled with His presence and become a manifestation of Christ to those around us. There is no greater way to live than to be carriers of God's Presence.

Concerning all believers: Blessed are those who hunger and thirst for righteousness, for they shall be filled.

Matthew 5:6 NKJV

Concerning Jesus as a boy: And the Child grew and became strong in spirit, filled with wisdom; and the grace of God was upon Him.

Luke 2:40 NKJV

Concerning John the Baptist: For he will be great in the sight of the Lord, and shall drink neither wine nor strong drink. He will also be filled with the Holy Spirit, even from his mother's womb.

Luke 1:15 NKJV

Concerning Elizabeth: And it happened, when Elizabeth heard the greeting of Mary, that the babe leaped in her womb; and Elizabeth was filled with the Holy Spirit.

Luke 1:41

Concerning the 120 followers of Christ on the Day of Pentecost: And suddenly there came a sound from heaven, as of a rushing mighty wind, and it filled the whole house where they were sitting. Then there appeared to them divided tongues, as of fire, and one sat upon each of them. And they were all filled with the Holy Spirit and began to speak with other tongues, as the Spirit gave them utterance.

Acts 2:2–4

And the testimony is this, that God has given us eternal life, and this life is in His Son. He who has the Son has the life; he who does not have the Son of God does not have the life.

1 John 5:11–12

37

HE WHO KNOWS EVERY HAIR ON OUR HEAD AND WHO NAMES EACH STAR

Are not five sparrows sold for two cents? Yet not one of them is forgotten before God. Indeed, the very hairs of your head are all numbered. Do not fear; you are more valuable than many sparrows.

Luke 12:6–7

Whether in creation or with His children, God is concerned with detail. Nothing escapes Him, and it is all for His purpose and for His glory. Especially important to Him are those who are related to Him through their acceptance of Christ. The Omniscient God understands everyone's heart and the way they think. Jesus said that He would not entrust Himself to man because He knew what was in man; yet His mercy is new every morning and for those who abandon themselves completely to Him will find unlimited supply for every good work.

He counts the number of the stars; He gives names to all of them.

Psalm 147:4

"I, Jesus, have sent My angel to testify to you these things for the churches. I am the root and the descendant of David, the bright and morning star."

Revelation 22:16

The name of the star is called Wormwood; and a third of the waters became wormwood, and many men died from the water, because they were made bitter.

Revelation 8:11

38

THE TENDER, PATIENT, ALL-ENCOMPASSING ONE, UPHOLDING ALL THINGS WITH HIS RIGHT HAND

The Lord is not slow about His promise, as some count slowness, but is patient toward you, not wishing for any to perish but for all to come to repentance.

2 Peter 3:9

God is gentle, kind and understands each one of us intimately, even though we might not know Him. Yes, that is the true! And His love for us is perfect. No one on Earth is like God. No one knows and loves us as God does. We can be changed into His likeness as we receive and walk in the light of His truth; His Word is truth. Lies will lead us away from God, but a person who loves truth will become more and more like Jesus.

But as many as received Him, to them He gave the right to become children of God, even to those who believe in His name, who were born, not of blood nor of the will of the flesh nor of the will of man, but of God.

John 1:12–13

And He is the radiance of His glory and the exact representation of His nature, and upholds all things by the word of His power. When He had made purification of sins, He sat down at the right hand of the Majesty on high.

Hebrews 1:3

39

THE CAPTAIN OF THE HEAVENLY HOSTS, THE MIGHTY WARRIOR

Now when Joshua was by Jericho, he looked up, and behold, a man was standing opposite him with his drawn sword in his hand, and Joshua went to him and said to him, "Are you for us or for our adversaries?" He said, "No; rather I have come now as captain of the army of the LORD." Then Joshua fell with his face toward the earth and bowed down, and said to him, "What does my lord have to say to his servant?" The captain of the LORD'S army said to Joshua, "Remove your sandals from your feet, because the place where you are standing is holy (set apart to the LORD)." And Joshua did so.

Joshua 5:13–15 AMP

God wars against anything that does not issue from love for His essence is love. He initiates life and sustains it. Life as God created it to be is superior to anything less than what He had originally intended. Death began its reign when Adam and Eve chose to disobey God's command and received the lie that came from the mouth of Satan in the form of a serpent. God's way is not our way; He wages war with truth. His Word is true and it brings enlightenment. All who live in agreement with lies oppose God and His truth either by ignorance or choice.

When those who are loyal to God speak truth in love, it can overpower any lie and bring forth revelation, which leads to Eternal Life. Christ partners with those who have chosen to live life with Him. Living in cooperation with God we are able to overcome every enemy of truth, righteousness and justice. This is the war we wage every day.

See now that I, I am He, And there is no god besides Me; It is I who put to death and give life. I have wounded, and it is I who heal; And there is no one who can deliver from My hand. Indeed, I lift up My hand to heaven, And say, as I live forever, If I sharpen My flashing sword, And My hand takes hold on justice, I will render vengeance on My adversaries, And I will repay those who hate Me.

Deuteronomy 32:39–41

The unfolding of Your words gives light; It gives understanding to the simple.

Psalm 119:130

And I saw heaven opened; and behold, a white horse, and He who sat upon it is called Faithful and True; and in righteousness He judges and wages war. And His eyes are a flame of fire, and upon His head are many diadems, and He has a name written upon Him which no one knows except Himself. And He is clothed with a robe dipped in blood; and His name is called The Word of God. And the armies which are in heaven, clothed in fine linen, white and clean, were following Him on white horses. And from His mouth comes a sharp sword, so that with it He may smite the nations; and He will rule them with a rod of iron; and He treads the wine press of the fierce wrath of God, the Almighty. And on His robe and on His thigh He has a name written, KING OF KINGS, AND LORD OF LORDS.

Revelation 19:11–16

40

OUR PASSOVER LAMB, SUBSTITUTE AND VICTORIOUS TRIUMPHANT ONE

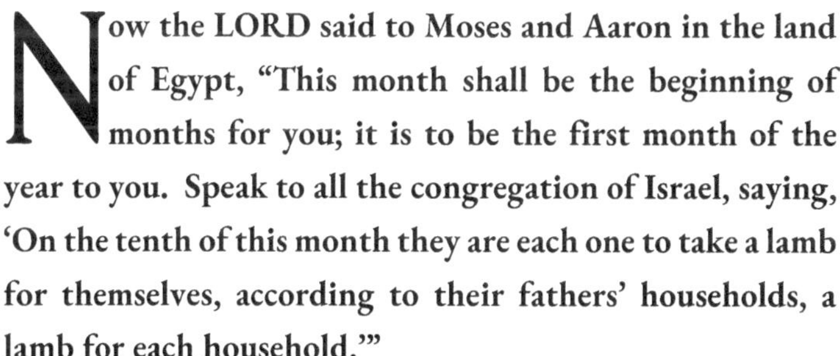

Now the LORD said to Moses and Aaron in the land of Egypt, "This month shall be the beginning of months for you; it is to be the first month of the year to you. Speak to all the congregation of Israel, saying, 'On the tenth of this month they are each one to take a lamb for themselves, according to their fathers' households, a lamb for each household.'"

Exodus 12:1–3

As we follow the history of the first Passover in Exodus to the last Passover before Jesus sacrificed His life, we see God's provision for the sin of humanity. The lamb offered for the sin of the people in the Old Testament was a picture of the Lamb of God, Messiah who was to come. Christ became our substitute as He suffered and died on Calvary's cross, paying the debt we could not pay to reconcile a people to His God and Father. Jesus rose from the dead conquering sin, death and the grave.

He lives forever in the presence of God interceding on behalf of humanity and all who believe in Him.

Your lamb shall be an unblemished male a year old; you may take it from the sheep or from the goats. And you shall keep it until the fourteenth day of the same month, then the whole assembly of the congregation of Israel is to kill it at twilight. Moreover, they shall take some of the blood and put it on the two doorposts and on the lintel of the houses in which they eat it.

Exodus 12:5-7

And the blood shall be a sign for you on the houses where you live; and when I see the blood I will pass over you, and no plague will befall you to destroy you when I strike the land of Egypt.

Exodus 12:13

Then came the first day of Unleavened Bread on which the Passover lamb had to be sacrificed. And He sent Peter and John, saying, "Go and prepare the Passover for us, that we may eat it."

Luke 22:7–8

So he then handed Him over to them to be crucified. They took Jesus, therefore, and He went out, bearing His own cross, to the place called the Place of a Skull, which is called in Hebrew, Golgotha. There they crucified Him, and with Him two other men, one on either side, and Jesus in between. Pilate also wrote an inscription and put it on the cross. It was written, "JESUS THE NAZARENE, THE KING OF THE JEWS."

John 19:16–19

When therefore it was evening, on that day, the first day of the week, and when the doors were shut where the disciples were for fear of the Jews, Jesus came and stood in their midst, and said to them, "Peace be with you." And when He had said this, He showed them both His hands and His side. The disciples therefore rejoiced when they saw the Lord. Jesus therefore said to them again, "Peace be with you, as the Father has sent Me, I also send you." And when He had said this, He breathed on them, and said to them, "Receive the Holy Spirit."

John 20:19–22

41

OUR JOYOUS OVERCOMING KING AND PRINCE OF PEACE

Peace I leave with you, My peace I give to you; not as the world gives, do I give to you. Do not let your heart be troubled, nor let it be fearful.

John 14:27

Jesus, the Prince of Peace, comes to live within us; therefore the peace that we need or desire already resides in God in us. Holy Spirit brings God's fullness; therefore we lack nothing. Learning the truth of this reality about God enables us to access everything His fullness offers. If we need peace, we look to Christ in us and yield to Him. As we let go of doubt, anxiety, unbelief, and fear, we let go of anything that would diminish, obstruct or oppose what is available to us through God and freedom will be experienced. Ask, seek, knock and continue in this until what is already available becomes manifest. God's supply is abundant. In Him there is no lack.

Therefore, since we have so great a cloud of witnesses surrounding us, let us also lay aside every encumbrance, and the sin which so easily entangles us, and let us run with endurance the race set before us, fixing our eyes on Jesus, the author and perfecter of faith, who for the joy set before Him endured the cross, despising the shame, and has sat down at the right hand of the throne of God. For consider Him who has endured such hostility by sinners against Himself, so that you may not grow weary and lose heart.

Hebrews 12:1–3

These things I have spoken to you while abiding with you. But the Helper, the Holy Spirit, whom the Father will send in My name, He will teach you all things, and bring to your remembrance all that I said to you. Peace I leave with you; My peace I give to you; not as the world gives do I give to you. Do not let your heart be troubled, nor let it be fearful.

John 14:25-27

42

HOPE OF THE NATIONS, KING ABOVE ALL KINGS, LORD ABOVE ALL LORDS, THE EXALTED ONE

All the ends of the earth will remember and turn to the LORD. And all the families of the nations will worship before Thee.

Psalm 22:27

The majesty of the King and Lord of all, who in humility took upon Himself the form of humanity, fulfilled the will of the Eternal God by becoming the sacrifice to purchase back God's creation. Christ is forever exalted in Heaven as the Overcomer for all who believe in Him; for all who embrace His Salvation and Lordship in their lives.

Co-laboring with Christ we become God's agents working to see His Kingdom established on Earth.

All nations whom Thou hast made shall come and worship before Thee, O Lord; And they shall glorify Thy name.

Psalm 86:9

And they sang the song of Moses the bond-servant of God and the song of the Lamb, saying,

"Great and marvelous are Your works,

O Lord God, the Almighty;

Righteous and true are Your ways,

King of the nations!

Who will not fear, O Lord, and glorify Your name?

For You alone art holy;

For ALL THE NATIONS WILL COME AND

WORSHIP BEFORE YOU, FOR YOUR RIGHTEOUS

ACTS HAVE BEEN REVEALED."

Revelation 15:3-4

And being found in appearance as a man, He humbled Himself by becoming obedient to the point of death, even death on a cross. Therefore also God highly exalted Him, and bestowed on Him the name which is above every name, that at the name of Jesus every knee should bow, of those who are in heaven, and on earth, and under the earth, and that every tongue should confess that Jesus Christ is Lord, to the glory of God the Father.

Philippians 3:8–11

43

THE ONE WHO GATHERS AND HE WHO SCATTERS IS THE SAME

Then the LORD your God will restore your fortunes (in return from exile), and have compassion on you, and will gather you together again from all the peoples (nations) where He has scattered you.

Deuteronomy 30:3 AMP

In the Old Testament, after repeated attempts to reason with them, God's people hardened their hearts and refused to listen to Him. Then He would allow them to be taken into exile by other nations. It was God's way of disciplining them for their repeated stubbornness and rebellion. While in the hands of enemy nations, the people of God would cry out to Him for deliverance. God, in His tender-hearted mercy, heard their cry and would answer their prayers. By providential dealings He would work to bring them back to their homeland. God would be faithful to the covenant He made with their forefathers. As Creator He would draw the hearts of His wayward people back into relationship with Him and bring them under the protection of His sovereignty.

Do not fear, for I am with you; I will bring your offspring from the east, And gather you from the west. I will say to the north, 'Give them up!' And to the south, 'Do not hold them back.' Bring My sons from afar And My daughters from the ends of the earth, Everyone who is called by My name, And whom I have created for My glory, Whom I have formed, even whom I have made."

Isaiah 43:5–8

44

HE WHO RAISES THE DEAD AND QUICKENS THE FAINTING ONE, OPENS BLIND EYES, UNPLUGS DEAF EARS AND MAKES A HEART OF STONE A HEART OF FLESH— HE NEVER TIRES OF DOING GOOD

I was blind to my sin and unable to see truth. I had no understanding of the depth of ignorance concerning God until the Holy Spirit began to reveal truth to me. A friend shared her testimony of encountering God, and I knew I wanted to know Him too. Holy Spirit was drawing me and I experienced spiritual experiences that brought me to surrender my life and to accept Christ as my Savior and Lord. Hunger for God's Word led me to join a women's Bible study group. I began to gain understanding about Jesus. Reading the Gospels led me to see that God the Father was just like Jesus, His Son. Jesus said, "He who has seen Me has seen the Father."

I began to read God's Word and talk to Him daily. I went to meetings when and wherever to learn more about God and experience His Presence.

Away at a women's retreat, I had conviction of my sin and a revelation of understanding that I needed a change of mind and heart. I was learning about repentance. I became very aware that my thinking had to change and agree with God's Word. My thoughts and actions were wrong; they were not like God's.

In His goodness, He was opening my blind eyes, and I was hearing Him speak to me. I learned to develop a hearing ear as I listened for His voice. Holy Spirit had such patience as He showed me His ways by correcting my faulty thinking and my fearful heart. One day, He spoke to me and said, "I will light your lamp, I will enlighten your darkness." There was darkness within me and God would reveal the truth of His ways so I would know how to turn from my old ways and be more like Jesus.

I was learning about my heavenly Father by studying the life of Jesus. The Holy Spirit of the Risen Christ, the third person of the Trinity, had become my teacher.

I was grateful for God's forgiveness, and I saw the truth of forgiving others as I had been forgiven by God. My heart and mind were being transformed. As a man thinks in his heart so is he. I had to meditate on that truth for a long time. My mind and heart were so connected that they both were going through transformation. The Holy Spirit worked within me as I received the Scriptures daily. Truth was overtaking lies that I had believed, light was overcoming the darkness, and the life of God was creating a new woman. A daughter whose character was becoming more like her Father's was changing little by little every day.

God's goodness continues to lead me into new life. I live by faith in the Son of God. His goodness is unsearchable and unending. He never tires of being good to all living beings. Perfect goodness flows from the pure heart of God's love. God is love; in Him there is no darkness at all. Everything He does is motivated by love and for love. We are loved by God. Picture Jesus on the cross in your mind; see His life's blood being poured out to pay the price for your sin, a price we were unable to pay, and you'll begin to experience the holy and pure love of God for you—personally for you. It was personal to God as He watched His Son suffer in humiliation and agony.

We all have the opportunity to personally respond to God's love in Jesus Christ. Have you realized and accepted God's divine love for you?

Jesus said, "Have I been so long with you, and yet you have not come to know Me, Philip? He who has seen Me has seen the Father; how can you say, 'Show us the Father'?"

John 14:9

For You light my lamp; The LORD my God illumines my darkness.

Psalm 18:28

Your word is a lamp to my feet and a light to my path.

Psalm 119:105

But when He, the Spirit of truth, comes, He will guide you into all the truth; for He will not speak on His own initiative, but whatever He hears, He will speak; and He will disclose to you what is to come.

John 16:13

And forgive us our sins, as we have forgiven those who sin against us.

Matthew 6:12 NLT

And that you be renewed in the spirit of your mind, and put on the new self, which in the likeness of God has been created in righteousness and holiness of the truth.

Ephesians 4:23–24

Remind them to be subject to rulers, to authorities, to be obedient, to be ready for every good deed, to malign no one, to be peaceable, gentle, showing every consideration for all men. For we also once were foolish ourselves, disobedient, deceived, enslaved to various lusts and pleasures, spending our life in malice and envy, hateful, hating one another. But when the kindness of God our Savior and His love for mankind appeared, He saved us, not on the basis of deeds which we have done in righteousness, but according to His mercy, by the washing of regeneration and renewing by the Holy Spirit, whom He poured out upon us richly through Jesus Christ our Savior, so that being justified by His grace we would be made heirs according to the hope of eternal life.

Titus 3:1–7

45

HE WILL NOT BE MOCKED

The LORD, the God of their fathers, sent word to them again and again by His messengers, because He had compassion on His people and on His dwelling place. But they kept mocking the messengers of God and despising His words and scoffing at His prophets until the wrath of the LORD arose against His people, until there was no remedy or healing.

2 Chronicles 36:15–16 AMP

God never does anything haphazardly. Everything He says and does is for a purpose. "The fear of the Lord is the beginning of wisdom," says God's Word. Fools despise correction and instruction, and in pride they disregard the one in whose image they are created. Oftentimes I hear about things men have done and I think that animals are wiser than humans. The instruction to man from God is not without consequences, good or evil. People will succeed or fail directly because of the choices they make. God is good and desires good for His creation. Those who honor and revere God and obey His Word will reap the rewards of His blessings. There is eternal wealth that can only come through obedience and cannot be purchased as a commodity. Material riches, on the other hand, whether acquired by hard work or deceit, have no lasting value. Once spent, they are gone.

The law of sowing and reaping will never end. As the Bible states, **"Sow with a view to righteousness, Reap in accordance with kindness; Break up your fallow ground, For it is time to seek the LORD Until He comes to rain righteousness on you."**

Hosea 10:12

Whoever mocks the poor taunts his Maker, And he who rejoices at (another's) disaster will not go unpunished.

Proverbs 17:5 AMP

Do not be deceived, God is not mocked (He will not allow Himself to be ridiculed, nor treated with contempt nor allow His precepts to be scornfully set aside); for whatever a man sows, this and this only is what he will reap. For the one who sows to his flesh (his sinful capacity, his worldliness, his disgraceful impulses) will reap from the flesh ruin and destruction, but the one who sows to the Spirit will from the Spirit reap eternal life.

Galatians 6:7–8 AMP

For as the heavens are higher than the earth, So are My ways higher than your ways And My thoughts than your thoughts. For as the rain and the snow come down from heaven, And do not return there without watering the earth And making it bear and sprout, And furnishing seed to the sower and bread to the eater; So will My word be which goes forth from My mouth; It will not return to Me empty, Without accomplishing what I desire, And without succeeding in the matter for which I sent it.

Isaiah 55:10–11

46

HE IS THE TRUTH

A nd the Word became flesh, and dwelt among us, and we saw His glory, glory as of the only begotten from the Father, full of grace and truth. For the law was given through Moses; grace and truth were realized through Jesus Christ.

John 1:14,17

If anyone wants to know truth that will give understanding to their heart, only the Spirit of Truth can reveal it. Pontius Pilate, governor of Rome, stood before Christ and asked, "What is truth?" He stood before the one Who said that He was the Truth and had an honest question.

What is your belief today? Have you come to meet Jesus face-to-face? Truth is not far from any one of us. You can ask Jesus the same question as Pilate. Everyone who seeks truth with their whole heart and soul will indeed find it. God will make

Himself known to every seeking heart; faith comes from the heart. God has given to each person a measure of faith. Exercise your faith. Overcome unbelief; silence every lie and disappointment and come to Jesus Christ. You will not be disappointed. He is the Good Shepherd waiting and longing to feed each hungry, seeking soul.

Pilate said to Him, "What is truth?"

John 18:38

Jesus said to him, 'I am the way, and the truth, and the life; no one comes to the Father but through Me.'

John 14:6

This is good and acceptable in the sight of God our Savior, who desires all men to be saved and to come to the knowledge of the truth. For there is one God, and one mediator also between God and men, the man Christ Jesus.

1 Timothy 2:3–5

The one who says, "I have come to know Him," and does not keep His commandments, is a liar, and the truth is not in him; but whoever keeps His word, in him the love of God has truly been perfected. By this we know that we are in Him: the one who says he abides in Him ought himself to walk in the same manner as He walked.

1 John 2:4–6

47

HE NEVER FAILS, HE'S ALREADY OVERCOME

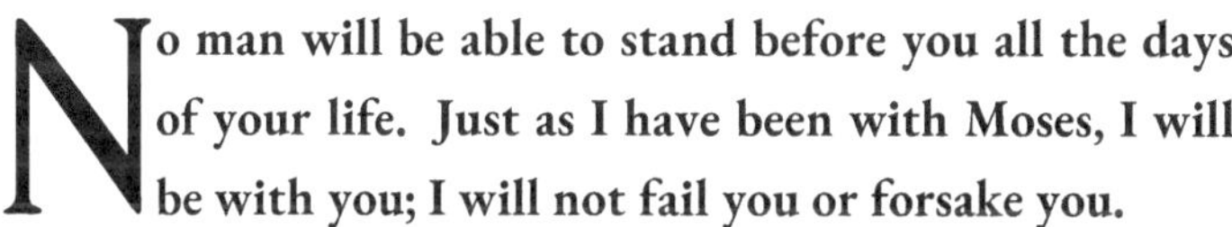

No man will be able to stand before you all the days of your life. Just as I have been with Moses, I will be with you; I will not fail you or forsake you.

Joshua 1:5

When I know who God is by the authority of His Word, I am not afraid to have faith in Him. Confidence in Christ's completed work and His character enables me to live above every fear. Jesus has already obtained the victory over sin, Satan and death. Those who have chosen to follow Him in obedience and unyielding devotion are recipients of His authority.

And Jesus came up and spoke to them saying, "All authority has been given to Me in heaven and on earth. Go therefore and make disciples of all the nations, baptizing them in the name of the Father and the Son and the Holy

Spirit, teaching them to observe all that I commanded you; and lo, I am with you always, even to the end of the age."

Matthew 28:18–20

These will wage war against the Lamb, and the Lamb will overcome them, because He is Lord of lords and King of kings, and those who are with Him are the called and chosen and faithful.

Revelation 17:14

He who overcomes, I will grant to him to sit down with Me on My throne, as I also overcame and sat down with My Father on His throne.

Revelation 3:21

For whatever is born of God overcomes the world; and this is the victory that has overcome the world—our faith. Who is the one who overcomes the world, but he who believes that Jesus is the Son of God? This is the One who came by water and blood, Jesus Christ; not with the water only, but with the water and with the blood. It is the Spirit who testifies, because the Spirit is the truth. For there are three that testify: the Spirit and the water and the blood; and the three are in agreement. If we receive the testimony of men, the testimony of God is greater; for the testimony of God is this, that He has testified concerning His Son.

1 John 5:4–9

48

HE IS THE ALPHA AND THE OMEGA, GIVING REST TO THE WEARY, THE LIVING HOPE

"**I am the Alpha and the Omega,**" says the Lord God, "**who is and who was and who is to come, the Almighty.**"

Revelation 1:8

He who is the Alpha and the Omega, the Beginning and the End, who was with God in the beginning of the creation of the earth, and who will be at the end of the age of the Gentiles has spoken and continues to speak to us today. The living eternal Word has no end. Jesus has said of Himself that He is the same yesterday, today, and forever (Hebrews 13:8). From beginning to end He is sovereign in the affairs of men. His desire has always been that His creation would honor and revere Him, obeying His commands so that they would have success. Yet over and over again, many of those He called and named to be His own, from

Israel of old to the church of Christian believers today, disobedience and compromise has put at a continual crossroad. If our hearts have been captured by God's sacrificial love in Christ and our lives are united to Him and His Word, we have a hope that will never fade or disappoint. The living peace because of Christ's indwelling presence is what gives stability to life and the choices we make. Prisoners of hope are those wrapped in the all-encompassing overcoming life of Christ. Believers are victorious in the finished work of Jesus.

Then He said to me, "It is done. I am the Alpha and the Omega, the beginning and the end. I will give to the one who thirsts from the spring of the water of life without cost."

Revelation 21:6

"Listen to Me, O Jacob, even Israel whom I called; I am He, I am the first, I am also the last. Surely My hand founded the earth, And My right hand spread out the heavens; When I call to them, they stand together. Assemble, all of you, and listen! Who among them has declared these things? The LORD loves him; he will carry out His good pleasure on Babylon, And His arm shall be against the Chaldeans. I, even I, have spoken indeed I have called him, I have brought him, and He will make his ways successful. Come near to Me, listen to this: From the first I have not spoken in secret, From the time it took place, I was there. And now the Lord GOD has sent Me, and His Spirit."

Isaiah 48:12–16

He gives strength to the weary, And to him who lacks might He increases power.

Isaiah 40:29

For who provoked Him when they had heard? Indeed, did not all those who came out of Egypt led by Moses? And with whom was He angry for forty years? Was it not with those who sinned, whose bodies fell in the wilderness? And to whom did He swear that they would not enter His rest, but to those who were disobedient? So we see that they were not able to enter because of unbelief.

Hebrews 3:16–19

Come to Me, all who are weary and heavy-laden, and I will give you rest.

Matthew 11:28

Blessed be the God and Father of our Lord Jesus Christ, who according to His great mercy has caused us to be born again to a living hope through the resurrection of Jesus Christ from the dead, to obtain an inheritance which is imperishable and undefiled and will not fade away, reserved in heaven for you, who are protected by the power of God through faith for a salvation ready to be revealed in the last time.

1 Peter 1:3–5

For it is for this we labor and strive, because we have fixed our hope on the living God, who is the Savior of all men, especially of believers.

1 Timothy 4:10

Now may the God of hope fill you with all joy and peace in believing, so that you will abound in hope by the power of the Holy Spirit.

Romans 15:13

49

HE GRIEVES, HE WEEPS, GETS ANGRY, REJOICES AND LAUGHS AT HIS ENEMIES

The LORD was sorry that He had made man on the earth, and He was grieved in His heart.

Genesis 6:6

God made man in His image and after His likeness. We are like God when we allow truthful emotions to be seen through us in various life encounters. Our heart motives must also agree with His so that what is expressed through our personality can be experienced by those around us. When Jesus saw the money-changers in the temple and merchants buying and selling, He became indignant. A righteous anger took hold of Him, and He manifested a zeal for His Father's house. He said to them, "It is written, 'And My house shall be a house of prayer,' but you have made it a robbers' den."

(Luke 19:46)

Then He said to them, "My soul is deeply grieved, to the point of death; remain here and keep watch with Me."

Matthew 26:38

When He approached Jerusalem, He saw the city and wept over it.

Luke 19:41

When Jesus therefore saw her weeping, and the Jews who came with her also weeping, He was deeply moved in spirit and was troubled, and said, "Where have you laid him?" They said to Him, "Lord, come and see." Jesus wept.

John 11:33–35

He said, "The LORD is my rock and my fortress and my deliverer;

My God, my rock, in whom I take refuge,

My shield and the horn of my salvation, my stronghold and my refuge;

My savior, You save me from violence.

I call upon the LORD, who is worthy to be praised,

And I am saved from my enemies.

For the waves of death encompassed me; The torrents of destruction overwhelmed me; The cords of Sheol surrounded me; The snares of death confronted me. In my distress I called upon the LORD,

Yes, I cried to my God; And from His temple He heard my voice,

And my cry for help came into His ears. Then the earth shook and quaked, The foundations of heaven were trembling And were shaken, because He was angry.

2 Samuel 22:2–9

You will also be a crown of beauty in the hand of the LORD, And a royal diadem in the hand of your God. It will no longer be said to you, "Forsaken," Nor to your land will it any longer be said, "Desolate"; But you will be called, "My delight is in her," And your land, "Married"; For the LORD delights in you, And to Him your land will be married. For as a young man marries a virgin, So your sons will marry you; And as the bridegroom rejoices over the bride, So your God will rejoice over you.

Isaiah 62:3–5

The kings of the earth take their stand And the rulers take counsel together Against the LORD and against His Anointed, saying, "Let us tear their fetters apart And cast away their cords from us!" He who sits in the heavens laughs, The Lord scoffs at them. Then He will speak to them in His anger And terrify them in His fury, saying, "But as for Me, I have installed My King Upon Zion, My holy mountain."

Psalm 2:2–6

50

THE SUN OF RIGHTEOUSNESS, THE MORNING STAR

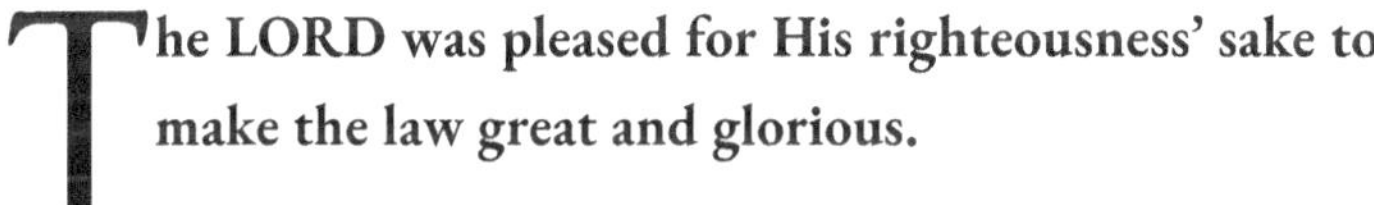

The LORD was pleased for His righteousness' sake to make the law great and glorious.

Isaiah 42:21

God who has no unrighteousness in Him gives His righteousness to those who accept His Son of whom it is said: "Who committed no sin, nor was any deceit found in His mouth." For those who have accepted Christ as Lord, the light of His righteousness arises in them to be seen in what they say and what they do. The One who causes the dawn to rise over the horizon of darkness, giving light to the day, is the same One who is seen within the lives of those aligned with Heaven and the purposes of the Kingdom of God and His Christ in the earth. Light overcomes darkness, and the darkness has no place to hide in the hearts of those who have chosen life over death and truth over lies. They are the stronghold of God in a world where the blind lead the blind and the truth is not found in them.

But for you who fear My name, the sun of righteousness will rise with healing in its wings; and you will go forth and skip about like calves from the stall.

Malachi 4:2

For in it the righteousness of God is revealed from faith to faith; as it is written, "But the righteous man shall live by faith."

Romans 1:17

But by His doing you are in Christ Jesus, who became to us wisdom from God, and righteousness and sanctification, and redemption.

1 Corinthians 1:30

So we have the prophetic word made more sure, to which you do well to pay attention as to a lamp shining in a dark place, until the day dawns and the morning star arises in your hearts.

2 Peter 1:19

He who overcomes, and he who keeps My deeds until the end, to him I will give authority over the nations; and he shall rule them with a rod of iron, as the vessels of the potter are broken to pieces, as I also have received authority from My Father; and I will give him the morning star.

Revelation 2:26–28

"I, Jesus, have sent My angel to testify to you and to give you assurance of these things for the churches. I am the Root (the Source, the Life) and the Offspring of David, the radiant and bright Morning Star."

Revelation 22:16 AMP

51

THE SON OF GOD, HIS NAME IS JESUS THE CHRIST, GOD'S MESSIAH, THE SENT ONE, THE PROPHET

Paul, a bond-servant of Christ Jesus, called as an apostle (special messenger, personally chosen representative), set apart for (preaching) the gospel of God (the good news of salvation), which He promised beforehand through His prophets in the sacred Scriptures—(the good news) regarding His Son, as to the flesh (His human nature), was born a descendant of David (to fulfill the covenant promises), and (as to His divine nature) according to the Spirit of holiness was openly designated to be the Son of God with power (in a triumphant and miraculous way) by His resurrection from the dead: Jesus Christ our Lord.

Romans 1:1–4 AMP

Jesus Christ fulfilled every Old Testament prophecy concerning the Messiah who was to come through the lineage of David to be the Savior of the world. He lived a sinless life, revealed His divinity by the countless miracles He performed, and conquered sin and death by rising from the dead. He was confirmed to be the Son of God by the witness of the voice of God. Many who heard believed; others doubted. Those who believed in Him received forgiveness of sin and the gift of eternal life.

The beginning of the gospel of Jesus Christ, the Son of God.

Mark 1:1

Now when all the people were baptized, that Jesus also was baptized, and while He was praying, heaven was opened, and the Holy Spirit descended upon Him in bodily form like a dove, and a voice came out of heaven, "You are My beloved Son, in You I am well-pleased."

Luke 3:21–22

Six days later Jesus took with Him Peter and James and John his brother, and led them up on a high mountain by themselves. And He was transfigured before them; and His face shone like the sun, and His garments became as white as light. And behold, Moses and Elijah appeared to them, talking with Him. Peter said to Jesus, "Lord, it is good for us to be here; if You wish, I will make three tabernacles here, one for You, and one for Moses, and one for Elijah." While he was still speaking, a bright cloud overshadowed

them, and behold, a voice out of the cloud said, "This is My beloved Son, with whom I am well pleased; listen to Him!"

Matthew 17:1–5

My brothers, have faith in our Lord Jesus Christ, the Lord of glory, without partiality.

James 2:1

For God so loved the world, that He gave His only begotten Son, that whoever believes in Him shall not perish, but have eternal life. For God did not send the Son into the world to judge the world, but that the world might be saved through Him.

John 3:16–17

Now the birth of Yeshua the Messiah happened this way: After His mother Miriam was engaged to Joseph, before they came together, she was found with child by the Holy Spirit.

Matthew 1:18 TSB

He who comes from above is above all. He who is of the earth is earthly and speaks of the earth. He who comes from heaven is above all. He bears witness of what He has seen and heard, yet no one receives His testimony. He who has received His testimony has certified that God is true. For He whom God has sent speaks the words of God, for God gives the Spirit without measure to Him. The Father loves the Son, and has placed all things into His hand.

John 3:31–35 TSB

This is eternal life: that they may know You, the only true God, and Yeshua the Messiah, whom You have sent.

John 17:3 TSB

52

HE WHO RESTORES THE SOUL, OUR HIGH PRIEST, THE PRIEST OF THE MOST-HIGH GOD, OUR REDEEMER

For there is one God, and one mediator also between God and men, the man Christ Jesus.

1 Timothy 2:5

Jesus is God's High Priest chosen to stand before Him on behalf of humanity. Those who have been redeemed by Christ's blood as payment for sin have the assurance of confidence before a holy God.

Jesus, as Priest of the Most-High God, stated, "It is finished," having completed the work God sent Him to accomplish.

Christ restores our soul, liberating it from sin and its effects as we walk in unbroken, faithful relationship with Him.

The **LORD** is my shepherd, I shall not want. He makes me lie down in green pastures; He leads me beside quiet waters. He restores my soul; He guides me in the paths of righteousness For His name's sake.

Psalm 23:1–3

Therefore, holy brethren, partakers of a heavenly calling, consider Jesus, the Apostle and High Priest of our confession. He was faithful to Him who appointed Him, as Moses also was in all His house.

Hebrews 3:1–2

The **LORD** has sworn and will not change His mind, You are a priest forever According the order of Melchizedek.

Psalm 110:4

For this Melchizedek, king of Salem, priest of the Most-High God, who met Abraham as he was returning from the slaughter of the kings and blessed him, to whom also Abraham apportioned a tenth part of all the spoils, was first of all, by the translation of his name, king of righteousness, and then also king of Salem, which is king of peace. Without father, without mother, without genealogy, having neither beginning of days nor end of life, but made like the Son of God, he remains a priest perpetually.

Hebrews 7:1–3

But now, thus says the LORD, your Creator, O Jacob, And He who formed you, O Israel, "Do not fear, for I have redeemed you; I have called you by your name you are Mine!"

Isaiah 43:1

Christ redeemed us from the curse of the Law, having become a curse for us—for it is written, "Cursed is everyone who hangs on a tree."

Galatians 3:13

53

THE WAY, THE TRUTH AND THE LIFE

D o not let your heart be troubled; believe in God, believe also in Me. In My Father's house are many dwelling places; if it were not so, I would have told you; for I go to prepare a place for you. If I go and prepare a place for you, I will come again and receive you to Myself, that where I am, there you may be also. And you know the way where I am going." Thomas said to Him, "Lord, we do not know where You are going, how do we know the way?" Jesus said to him, "I am the way, and the truth, and the life; no one comes to the Father but through Me."

John 14:1–6

All the paths of the LORD are lovingkindness and truth

To those who keep His covenant and His testimonies.

Psalm 25:10

Teach me Your way, O LORD; I will walk in Your truth; Unite my heart to fear Your name.

Psalm 86:11

Then Jesus arrived from Galilee at the Jordan coming to John, to be baptized by him. But John tried to prevent Him, saying, "I have need to be baptized by You, and do You come to me?" But Jesus answering said to him, "Permit it at this time; for in this way it is fitting for us to fulfill all righteousness." Then he permitted Him.

Matthew 3:13–15

This is eternal life, that they may know You, the only true God, and Jesus Christ whom You have sent.

John 17:3

For the wages of sin is death, but the free gift of God is eternal life in Christ Jesus our Lord.

Romans 6:23

But the path of the righteous is like the light of dawn,

That shines brighter and brighter until the full day.

The way of the wicked is like darkness;

They do not know over what they stumble.

My son, give attention to my words;

Incline your ear to my sayings.

Do not let them depart from your sight;

Keep them in the midst of your heart.

For they are life to those who find them,

And health to all their body.

Watch over your heart with all diligence,

For from it flow the springs of life.

Proverbs 4:18–23

May the Light of the World illumine the path of your life.

May the power of Truth liberate your heart by the glory of His Presence.

May the Lord of Life lead you by His great grace to the unending way of eternity found in the person of our Savior and Lord, Jesus Christ.

"All authority has been given to Me in heaven and on earth. Go therefore and make disciples of all the nations, baptizing them in the name of the Father and the Son and the Holy Spirit, teaching them to observe all that I commanded you; and lo, I am with you always, even to the end of the age." Jesus

Matthew 28:18–20

SECTION V

No Division in the Godhead

Unity is the trait of the Godly. Perfect unity is where one part fits perfectly with another. My heart desires oneness in My body; each part perfectly fitted together with another. As I create and make each member whole, one person is just as important as another; each different yet needed to make it complete. The shape, the look, the feel is different, yet the substance at the core is the same. Diversity in unity. Different and yet the same because of the root system. The core is what connects. The focus may be different, yet the goal the same. Oneness in purpose working together as precision in motion—all parts functioning together as one. Only unity can bring glory to the Creator as He intended.

I carefully labor over each part so that it will fit and function within the whole. When creating, a craftsman works on each piece separately with the intention of fitting it into the finished product. So it is with each member of My Body, the Church. Each piece is different from another, no two are alike. Yet at the core, the essence is the same; the substance of the Living God, "Immanuel—God with us." Personalities, abilities, gifts and callings fashion the creative form of each. The purpose of every member is different, yet the ability to fit together perfectly is present when the core value is love.

Each creation holds the value given to it by God. The purpose is different, yet the value is equal. Shape and form are different, the value is the same. There is no partiality with God. Value is given each part.

In Me there is no strife, no enmity. There is perfect peace within God who created and called every living thing to life. My desire for unity within My house will never diminish; it is My passion.

In Heaven there exists perfect unity; all moves in harmony. In Heaven everyone knows what is expected of them, and everyone does what is expected. There is unity at the core; there is no possibility of division. Rebellion cannot dwell in Heaven. Every tiny part is invaluable as related to the life of God who holds all together.

There is no lack in God who is the All-Sufficient One. The complete essence of His being is beyond our full understanding, yet we can know Him. Only our opposition can hinder full union; like constriction restricts full flow.

The Holy One operates in perfect union. Each part in its perfection motivates and fuels the motion of the whole on Earth as it is in Heaven. This is My desire. You lack no good thing. All has been amply given. There is abundance in unity.

What is it that you lack? Have I not given you all you need? Even becoming as you are in Christ that you may become as I am. I have given all. I have given Myself in the person of My Son. I have held nothing back that you might experience My perfection and be changed, bearing My image on Earth even as I am in Heaven.

He makes the whole body fit together perfectly. As each part does its own special work, it helps the other parts grow, so that the whole body is healthy and growing and full of love.

Ephesians 4:16 NLT

Then make me truly happy by agreeing wholeheartedly with each other, loving one another, and working together with one mind and purpose.

Philippians 2:2 NLT

For even as the body is one and yet has many members, and all the members of the body, though they are many, are one body, so also is Christ. For by one Spirit we were all baptized into one body, whether Jews or Greeks, whether slaves or free, and were all made to drink of one Spirit. For the body is not one member, but many.

I Corinthians 12:12–14

Now to Him who is able to do far more abundantly beyond all that we ask or think, according to the power that works within us, to Him be the glory in the church and in Christ Jesus to all generations forever and ever. Amen.

Ephesians 3:20–21

God, after He spoke long ago to the fathers in the prophets in many portions and in many ways, in these last days has spoken to us in His Son, whom He appointed heir of all things, through whom also He made the world. And He is the radiance of His glory and the exact representation of His nature, and upholds all things by the word of His power.

Hebrews 1:1–3a

Behold, how good and how pleasant it is

For brothers to dwell together in unity!

It is like the precious oil upon the head,

Coming down upon the beard,

Even Aaron's beard,

Coming down upon the edge of his robes.

It is like the dew of Hermon,

Coming down upon the mountains of Zion;

For there the LORD commanded the blessing—life forever.

Psalm 133

SECTION VI

THE WIND IN THE STORM

he source of My life comes as the wind; suddenly I am there.[1]

The Wind blows, the atmosphere shifts, change occurs. You can feel the wind yet you cannot know where it came from. Gently upon your face you sense the Presence; you feel it's nearness. Faith is stirring deep within you. The unseen yet gently felt breeze awakens within a longing. Night and day you wait listening for the faint stirrings of the One who suddenly is felt. The wind blows, sometimes faintly, other times as a violent storm. Yet peace is felt and then desire is awake.

How can this newfound Presence bring such change within? A deep sense of security from this unseen yet ever-present gentle One becomes a refuge, a retreat in the chaos of your surroundings. Circumstances whip at your face. You fear your next breath. Can you still breathe? How can you stand? Your strength fails you. Yet you remember the gentle breeze that brought such sweet quiet. Your heart turns. You are embraced by God. Your breathing calms; your heart is at rest. The Wind catches you up into a strong embrace. You are safe in the center of the storm.

---

[1] Jehovah-Shammah: Jehovah is there.

The gentle yet strong ever-present One who drew you away from the familiar has become your place of safety. "You can rest, assured of the strength of My Presence." Not always felt, yet near is the unseen One who has become a companion. He awakened your desire to know Him, the One who suddenly appears transcending time and space.

Life continues. Situations may change in turbulent, often uncertain existence, yet the place created by the Wind is your stronghold... The storm of life blows, bending you to breaking point, yet the mystery is there is a Wind that sustains and maintains your life. Your whole being has become rooted in this unseen faithful One.

There is the wind of the storm, fierce, frightening, robbing your breath. Fear of life and sanity looms heavy. Then at the same time there is the Wind in the storm, also fierce and powerful to keep your heart and faith from being crushed. Your fear is vanquished by the Wind in the storm. Yes it is true. The wind that came to rob and to destroy has been overcome by the Wind of vindication and victory.

You are safe. Your soul is at rest sheltered in the place forged by the winds of adversity. In the secret place within, the storm rages all around, yet safety is realized. The One who came to you suddenly and unseen made you to trust and be at peace. Oh, what blessed rest; You are renewed as deep quiet refreshes and strengthens you.

The Wind sees. The Wind knows. You anticipate His coming. Strength that comes from God assures you. Confident, now you can be at peace. Your understanding of the Wind's coming is evasive. You can feel it; then it is gone.

Yet a deposit of substance is left within, which has changed you forever.

As an anchor in the storm, the Wind has become the compass. Gently at times, forcefully at other times the Wind moves you along life's road; leading, teaching, comforting on this uncertain journey. The eye of the Wind is always upon you.

One day, when you thought the storm would destroy your life, this fresh Wind appeared, quiet yet strong. He captured your heart and saved you. In the middle of the storm a greater Wind appeared and drew you from the grip of fear to the place of peace. Forever united in trust, you move forward unafraid for you are not alone.

When unforeseen and crushing events invade our lives, even normal daily responsibilities can be overwhelming. Despair, disappointment and discouragement permeate, draining our hope and robbing the blessing each day has to offer. That is when the cry of the heart has the opportunity to reach Heaven's door. The way into the chamber of God's holy place is moved by the words we speak or the thoughts of our heart that cannot be expressed. Christ is listening. The Savior is ready to dispatch the resource of His Presence. The Wind of the unseen Holy Spirit of God makes Himself known to us revealing the power of His Kingdom on Earth.

The wind blows where it wishes and you hear the sound of it, but do not know where it comes from and where it is going; so is everyone who is born of the Spirit.

John 3:8

Do you not know that you are the temple of God and that the Spirit of God dwells in you? If anyone defiles the temple of God, God will destroy him. For the temple of God is holy, which temple you are.

1 Corinthians 3:16–17 NKJV

I will ask the Father, and He will give you another Helper, that He may be with you forever; that is the Spirit of truth, whom the world cannot receive, because it does not see Him or know Him, but you know Him because He abides with you and will be in you.

John 14:16–17

He who dwells in the shelter of the Most-High Will abide in the shadow of the Almighty. I will say to the LORD, "My refuge and my fortress, My God, in whom I trust!" For it is He who delivers you from the snare of the trapper And from the deadly pestilence. He will cover you with His pinions, And under His wings you may seek refuge; His faithfulness is a shield and bulwark. You will not be afraid of the terror by night, Or of the arrow that

flies by day; Of the pestilence that stalks in darkness, Or of the destruction that lays waste at noon.

Psalm 91:1–6

But if the Spirit of Him who raised Jesus from the dead dwells in you, He who raised Christ Jesus from the dead will also give life to your mortal bodies through His Spirit who dwells in you.

Romans 8:11

SECTION VII

THE CALM AFTER THE STORM

Such quiet. What fear. My soul reels from the storm. My heart questions, "Is there any purpose now? What remains? Is anything left?" Devastation is consuming my senses. "Where can I go to escape the terror?" My breath fails me, yet I am not alone. That familiar still small voice remains "Do not fear, I am with you. I will not leave you."

The winds of adversity blew over my world. I said to myself, "I am finished. What reason is there to go on? Everything is gone; nothing will ever be the same. How could this have happened? What purpose is there now in life?" My heart could find no reason to live. My eyes fixed upon the stillness, that deep quiet. "Is everything lost completely?"

Questions unending battered my mind; my heart had no strength. Again I hear from a place so deep I wonder if it is real. "I am with you. I will help you. Do not be afraid."

My heart continues to consider, "Is there any purpose, any reason to live?" Others also question, "Where do we begin to build?"

I remember God's comforting words that I am not alone, He will help me. God who is above all gods can take me past this moment and restore my purpose. Yes, hope is still alive. Creator-God who formed the universe sees and understands. God will help me to know how to rebuild. No, all is not lost. Hope is giving me strength, a resolve.

Life continues. There is purpose for there is breath.

Has He not said, "I am the way and the truth and the life"? In Him is life and the life is the light of men. The shattered pieces of the life I had known seemed hopeless. Yet, day after day God's voice gives me reason to believe again. All is not lost. I am alive and I am not forgotten. My lack of understanding gives way to His every Word. Emptiness craves to be satisfied. I am hungry for all that Holy Spirit speaks to me. Apart from Him and His Word there is no reason for breath. God alone is my help. He will not fail me

Jesus becomes my light in the darkness of truth. Reality slaps a blow that sends me reeling, but I am not alone. I am standing, and I have purpose. All is not lost. Many have lost hope and their pit is very deep. Their mind fails, and it seems that chaos has prevailed

Watching over the ashes of broken dreams is the One who is still with me, with you: The God who gives hope to the living and meaning to life. Apart from Him we can do nothing, but with Him, safely hidden in Him, drawing life from His unending love, hope is alive.

He whispers, His Presence enfolding me, "Am I not enough?"

"Yes", my heart agrees. "Yes, LORD, You're enough!"

My flesh and my heart may fail, but God is the strength of my heart and my portion forever.

Psalm 73:26

God is not a man, that He should lie, Nor a son of man, that He should repent; Has He said, and will He not do it? Or has He spoken, and will He not make it good?

Numbers 23:19

But the Helper, the Holy Spirit, whom the Father will send in My name, He will teach you all things, and bring to your remembrance all that I said to you.

John 14:26

Make sure that your character is free from the love of money, being content with what you have; for He Himself has said, "I will never desert you, nor will I ever forsake you."

Hebrews 13:5

TWO BY TWO

D o two people walk together, if they have not agreed?

Amos 3:3 MEV

There is a certain dynamic when two people are joined. It may be in friendship, marriage, business, community service, etc. Sharing life with another has a quality that cannot be experienced when you are alone in the natural life as well as the supernatural. Life dynamics can be positive and beneficial or negative, stressful and problematic.

The benefit of relationship with the risen Christ becomes clearer as that relationship develops over time. The many promises God gives to those who have been adopted by Him through faith in Christ are given so we become partakers of His divine nature. Being able to overcome the temptations that would cause us to compromise God's Word and bring reproach to His character makes us a clearer representation of who God is.

Also, as He goes before us preparing our path, He will reveal to us the pitfalls that pride can use to ensnare us. Since Jesus said that He is the light of the world, those who walk through life with

Him as Savior, companion, and Lord make a daily choice to align with truth according to Scripture.

The Apostle John said of Jesus, "The Word gave life to everything that was created, and His life brought light to everyone. The light shines in the darkness, and the darkness can never extinguish it."

John 1:4–5 NLT

Learning to reject what is false and being faithful to what is right and true according to God's word qualifies you to be an expression of God's heart. God's life is reproduced in you just as it was in Christ. As Jesus said, "I am to be no longer in the world, though these are in the world, for I am coming to You, Holy Father, through Your name keep those whom You have given Me, that they may be one as We are one."

John 17:11 MEV

For by these He has granted to us His precious and magnificent promises, so that by them you may become partakers of the divine nature, having escaped the corruption that is in the world by lust.

2 Peter 1:4

For you were once darkness, but now you are light in the Lord. Walk as children of light (for the fruit of the Spirit is in all goodness, righteousness, and truth), finding out what is acceptable to the Lord.

And have no fellowship with the unfruitful works of darkness, but rather expose them.

Ephesians 5:8–11 NKJV

Do not be bound together with unbelievers; for what partnership have righteousness and lawlessness, or what fellowship has light with darkness?

2 Corinthians 6:14

My sheep hear My voice, and I know them, and they follow Me.

John 10:27

There is no fear in love; but perfect love casts out fear, because fear involves torment. But he who fears has not been made perfect in love.

1 John 4:18

"Making your book dream come true
without robbing you!"

www.deeperlifepress.com